DESIGN FOR MODERN MERCHANDISING

DESIGN FOR MODERN MERCHANDISING

AN ARCHITECTURAL RECORD BOOK

Stores
Shopping Centers
Showrooms

PUBLISHED BY F. W. DODGE CORPORATION, NEW YORK

CONTENTS and notice of prior copyrights

(See also index, pages 243-247.)

(Continued on page v)

Contents and notice of prior copyrights (continued)

SECTION II—SHOPPING CENTERS

SECTION III—SHOWROOMS

INTRODUCTION

As this goes to press, Department of Commerce figures show retail sales close to an all-time high, with more persons engaged in wholesale and retail trade than ever before. Expanded merchandising activity is reflected in an unprecedented volume of planning and building of stores, shopping centers and showrooms. That this will continue is indicated by our continuing population growth and the long-range strength of the economy.

Thus this is a timely book. It deals with a very live subject—one engaging the talents of many architects and engineers and the considerable capital of many investors. It is our expectation that this volume will be helpful to both the designers and owners of today's—and tomorrow's—great output of architecture for selling.

It is not widely enough realized that complete and competent architectural design service is worth far more than the professional fee it costs. Its tangible benefits show up in greater sales, easier maintenance, more flexible use, higher rental or resale value and warmer public regard for the buildings themselves. Beyond that, good store design serves everyone by improving the marketplace environment, making shopping a more pleasant experience and the whole community more attractive.

It is hoped that this book, by presenting a wide selection of well designed stores, shopping centers and showrooms, skillfully photographed, will aid the reader by showing him by both picture and text how others have realized the plus values of good architecture for modern merchandising.

James S. Hornbeck

James S. Hornbeck, A.I.A.
Senior Associate Editor
Architectural Record

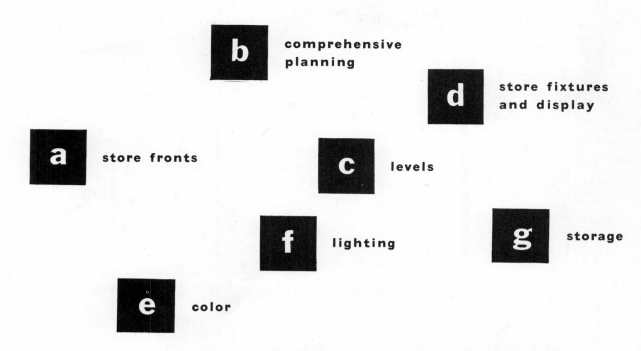

b comprehensive planning

d store fixtures and display

a store fronts

c levels

f lighting

g storage

e color

STORE DESIGN

by Caleb Hornbostel, Architect

THE NEWEST RELAXATION in the basic construction order by the National Production Authority this month is expected to add much to stimulate the field of store construction. For this reason and also because store design has gone through a complete overhauling in the postwar years, now — the middle of 1952 — is a good time to view in retrospect what the trends, directions and innovations have been and where they may be going.

Starting with the store front, we can obviously see that the open front has become an accepted formula except in the few cases where a store by its very nature can afford the closed front type of design. The open front has raised a host of design problems which did not exist before, namely, reflection, sun glare and sun control, new methods of window display, artificial lighting both day and night, a general reorganization of merchandise within the completely exposed store, together with a new approach to the design of display fixtures and casework in general.

In comprehensive planning of stores the most important consideration is circulation of customer traffic within the store. In planning suburban stores, which exist by serving the car shopper, parking facilities have become one of the major design factors. Parking facilities within the city are also a primary factor, but the solution to this problem goes beyond the usual field of store design and enters into that of civic planning.

A freer handling of levels within stores is one of the newer trends in store planning.

The whole field of display and casework is still in a state of change. The tendency is toward complete flexibility of fixtures and display, with the result that the store is becoming more and more of a stage set which adjusts to seasons, sales volume and buying trends.

Color has become a useful tool in store design. The psychological effects of color and its integration with lighting and display are being closely studied at present, indicating more use of color in the future.

Perhaps the greatest strides and innovations have taken place in store lighting. Lighting has now become an integral part of all comprehensive planning. Not only has general interior lighting changed, but, with the open store front, day and night lighting throughout the store has also become very important. The store sign enters the lighting problem and it, too, must be integrated into the design as a whole.

In store design the internal business operation of the store itself demands integrated storage of stock. There are three accepted methods of approaching this problem: (1) self-selection, where the majority of stock is on the actual sales floor and only remote storage is necessary; (2) all stock is concealed; and (3) multiple types of storage — exposed stock in showcases with some concealed stock, and reserve stock adjacent to the selling area.

Each of these aspects of store design has been treated separately and includes the opinions of a number of architects active in the field.

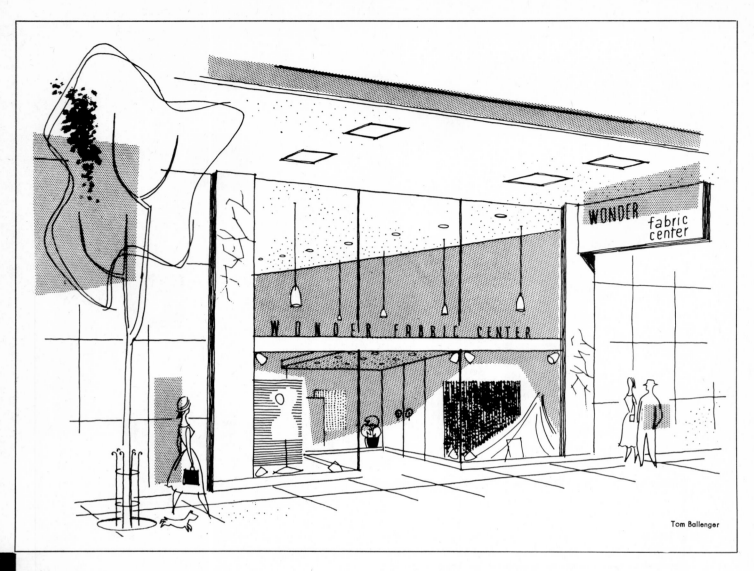

Tom Ballenger

store fronts

Roger Sturtevant

"THE STORE FRONT is the silent salesman working on the street 24 hours a day. It is newspaper advertising plastered across Main Street. Few indeed are the shops that are entered through a self-effacing door. These shops are the ones that have established a reputation for exclusiveness and customer selectivity which marks them as the extreme minority in the retail field. Mr. and Mrs. America and their children have been educated to shopping habits in which the store front plays a stellar role. Window shopping is probably the greatest single pastime of men, women and children throughout the country. Millions of dollars a year are spent on window display, and retailers today are much too canny to spend their money on anything which does not produce ample return on investment. To my mind, store fronts are the catalysts which turn window shoppers into customers and as such are a vital part of the retailer's selling equipment. As an architect who has spent many years in the store field, I feel that nothing contributes more to the quick and continued recognition of a retailing establishment by the public than the store front."

Morris Lapidus

Above: Thos. Tenney Shop, Berkeley, Calif.; Roger Lee, Architect

Courtesy of the Kawneer Co.

Gottscho-Schleisner

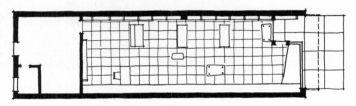

Above: The Little Shop, Niles, Mich.; Ketcham, Giná & Sharp, Architects. Door set at right angle gives total glass front area for display. Right: plan and photo, Wally Frank Ltd., New York City; Morris Lapidus, Architect. Below: The Rusk Shop Building in Houston, Tex., by MacKie and Kamrath, Architects, is a successful design for unified store group

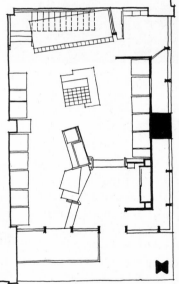

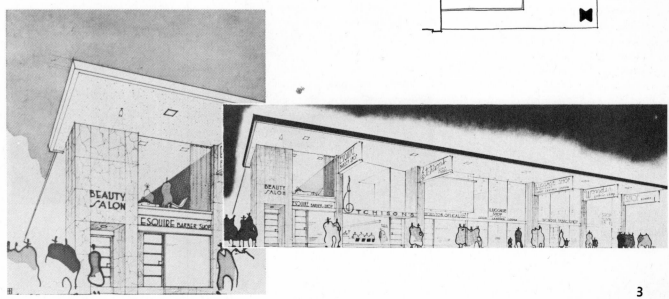

store fronts

Roger Sturtevant

Cargoes Inc., San Francisco, Calif.; Skidmore, Owings & Merrill, Architects; John L. King, Partner in charge; Don R. Knorr, Designer

The store itself acts as a showcase: its entire contents are the window display. Color and simple baffle walls are cleverly used to subdivide the space into various departments, yet allow the windowshopper to see into almost the full depth of the store. Yellow, a soft brown and orange-red predominate. Each color is used in relation to the merchandise which will be displayed against it. The photo to the right shows an interesting use of stock light fixtures. The casework is noteworthy for simplicity of design

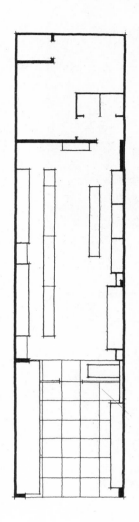

Above: Renee's Flower Shop, Beverly Hills, Calif.; Paul R. Williams, Architect; Robert Kliegman, Associate Architect. Overhang shades front, controls glare. Outdoor planting boxes help identify shop

Below: Dabby Shop, New York, N. Y.; Seymour R. Joseph, Architect. Display cases along sides of deeply set-in entrance lead passerby into store (see plan, left)

George M. Cushing, Jr.

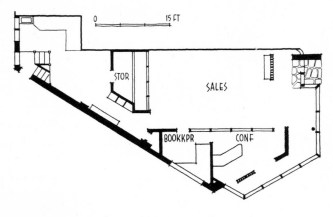

Above: Rogers Flower Shop, Brookline, Mass.; William Riseman Associates, Designers. Alteration opens up shop, gives identity

George M. Cushing, Jr.

E. A. Conrad Co., Beverley, Mass.; Constantin A. Pertzoff and Louisa V. Conrad, Associated Architects. Shop serves two age groups, each with separate sales areas. Slanting bay windows reduce sky reflection

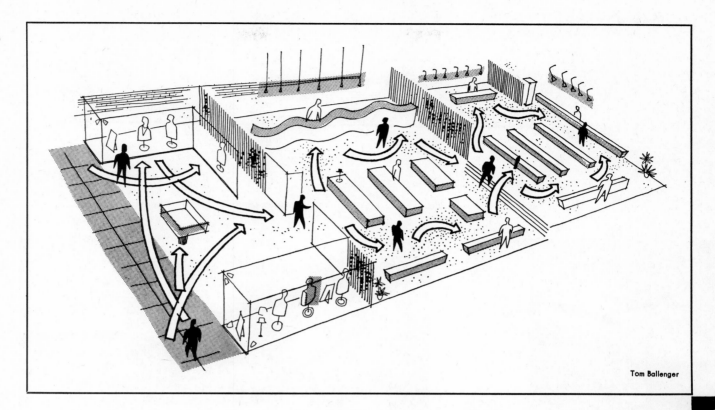

Tom Ballenger

comprehensive planning

b

Circulation

Departmental organization

Parking facilities

"The first step in comprehensive planning for small stores is setting up a program of overall requirements. This requires all the steps of research, survey and planning skill that one uses in programing the design of any complicated public project and consists of: a study of the needs, habits and buying potential of the public in the area; the ratio of dollar volume of yearly business to sales area to be occupied by various types of merchandise within the store; and, finally, the business background, philosophy and aptitude of the merchant who is to operate the store. The architect can then begin to intelligently plan the store and to interpret this data into proper area and volume allocations of the store. He must also provide for non-selling functions which are essential to proper customer service, comfort and store operation. This includes proper control of interior lighting and temperature. The last step is to promulgate a final layout for the store, based on a certain degree of flexibility in the plan and fixture details to provide for changes in buying trends, population shifts and other unpredictable factors which may affect business."

Daniel Schwartzman

"The most important factor in the existence of the suburban store and the one probably most closely related to sales is more and better parking facilities. Indeed, a new suburban store which does not provide these is extremely vulnerable to present and future competition and therefore represents a poor investment. Here are some criteria of what constitutes ample and convenient parking: a sufficient number of parking stalls as related to expected shopping volume rather than area of the store. It can be roughly estimated that one parking stall should be provided for a business volume of $8,000 to $12,000. Self parking shall be easy; angle parking is preferable. Parking stalls shall be of ample width and depth so that car doors can be opened and merchandise stored without hitting the neighboring car. Parking lots shall be well surfaced, clearly marked and well lit for night business. Landscaping and trees should be introduced to avoid a bleak appearance; these shall be well curbed or raised. Service traffic (deliveries, garbage collection) shall be strictly separated physically and visually from customer areas. Parking should be free."

Victor Gruen

comprehensive planning

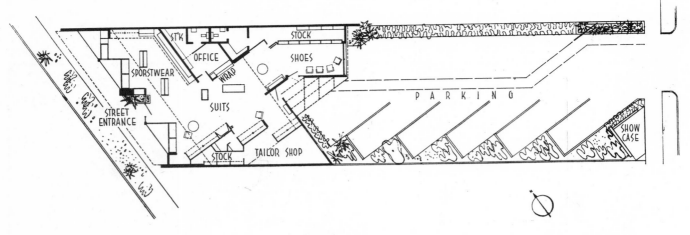

Stan Hall, Los Angeles, Calif.; Victor Gruen Associates, Architects; Rudi Baumfeld, Designer

Garber Sturges

Store layout uses full depth of irregularly shaped city block. It fronts on both streets, with parking lot entrance as important as sidewalk entrance. Interior circulation is controlled by clever use of baffling

Bettendorf's Market, Clayton, Mo.; Kenneth E. Wishmeyer, Architect

This supermarket with front and side parking features clear spans, clean-looking sanitary materials, incandescent lighting, summer or winter ventilation, well proportioned interiors. Noise control, ease of maintenance, pleasing color are other plus items. Materials handling was a prime design consideration

Arteaga Photos

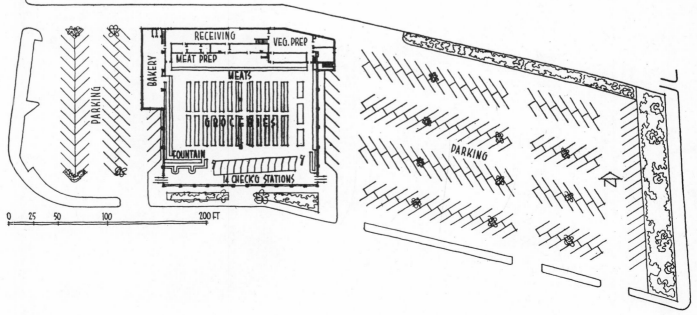

Roger Sturtevant

DIAGONAL WALLS CONTROL INTERNAL CIRCULATION

Thos. Tenney, Music on Records

Berkeley, Calif.

Roger Lee, Architect

INTERNAL space is quite confined in width as well as depth, yet the architect handled the space so cleverly that the customer is not aware that it is really very small. Location of the LP record rack opposite the listening booths makes for easy customer selection. Use of acoustical material on both ceiling and floor add to customer comfort. In the demonstration room at the back, a customer can relax and listen to various combinations of equipment and recording devices.

STOCK

DEMONSTRATION

BOOTH

BOOTH

BOOTH

SALES

STOR

0   10 FT.

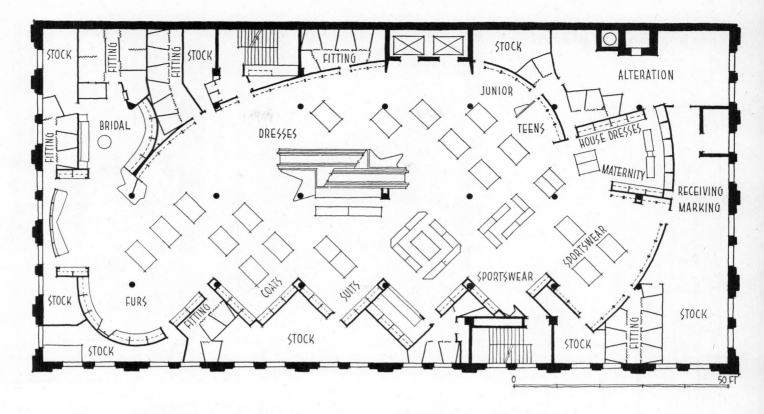

MERCHANDISING SEQUENCE DETERMINES LAYOUT

THIS PLAN SHOWS, to quote the architect, a logical sequence of customer traffic, starting near the highest traffic area with merchandise that has quick appeal, high unit profit and fast turnover and is bought on *impulse*, then proceeding with location of other merchandise lending itself to related selling or logical association, then to areas which ordinarily get the least traffic and to merchandise which is scarce or staple and therefore is bought on *demand*.

Trask, Prescott and Richardson

Erie, Pa.

Daniel Schwartzman, Architect

Meyers and Krider, Associated Architects

David Royter

comprehensive planning

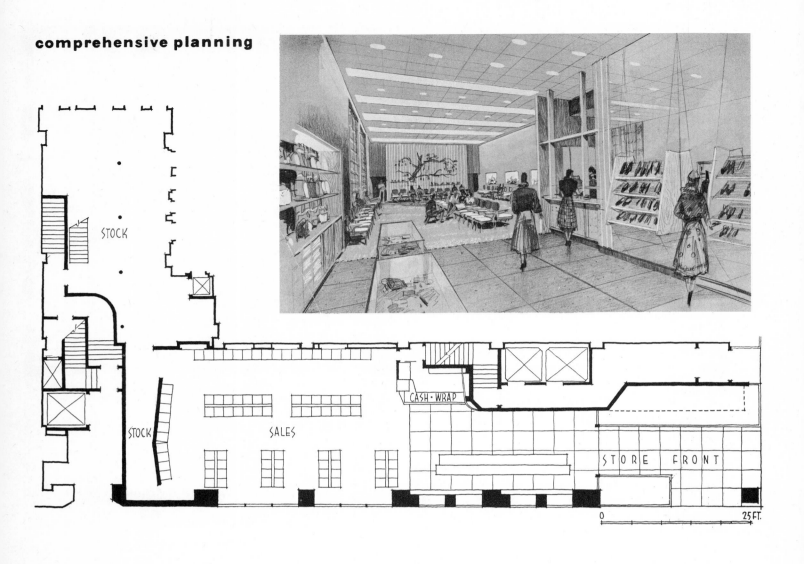

View from men's shop shows full depth of store. Floor racks of black wrought iron repeat design of other fixtures. Wall paneling is of juanacosta, floor is brick and tile. Color scheme is blue, cocoa brown and beige

A SIMPLE FLEXIBLE LAYOUT

Miles Shoes, New York, N. Y.
Furno and Harrison, Architects

THE PROBLEM was to not discourage low income sales by an overplush interior. The floor plan features three areas — display in store front area, intermediate area for accessories and impulse buying, and main sales area. Stock is kept off to one side, the entrance to it concealed by a decorative baffle wall in the rear. Mirrors increase the apparent width of the front area. Flexibility is the keynote of both sales areas. Lighting and cases hanging on mirror wall are interesting details.

STORE WITH TWO ENTRANCES

Foreman and Clark, Los Angeles, Calif.
Welton Becket and Associates, Architects

SEPARATE men's and women's departments are incorporated within the confines of a narrow rectangular site. Both entrances, one on Wilshire Boulevard and the other opening onto the parking lot, are given equal importance. The store is divided in the center by dressing rooms and executive offices. Distinction between men's and women's departments is further emphasized by using different decorative and color schemes. Area limitations are circumvented by an open merchandising plan. Floating racks of stainless steel suspended from the ceiling by wrought iron members, floor racks, and egg-crate counter fixtures are all light in design to increase feeling of space.

Above: women's department is carpeted; fixtures are pastel woods rather than wrought iron, and colors, including yellow and turquoise, are more feminine than in the men's department

Julius Shulman

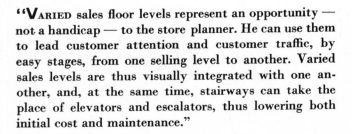

Tom Ballenger

C levels

"**V**ARIED sales floor levels represent an opportunity — not a handicap — to the store planner. He can use them to lead customer attention and customer traffic, by easy stages, from one selling level to another. Varied sales levels are thus visually integrated with one another, and, at the same time, stairways can take the place of elevators and escalators, thus lowering both initial cost and maintenance."

Morris Ketchum, Jr.

"**E**VEN in supermarkets, where single level operations, other than help's lockers and toilets, restrooms, boiler rooms, compressor rooms and similar units of this type, are the most efficient and inexpensive when site adequacy permits, there are many successful (financially) examples of two-level operations."

Kenneth Wishmeyer

Gottscho-Schleisner

Balch Price Store, Brooklyn, N.Y.
José A. Fernandez, Architect

NEW TRENDS IN THE USE OF LEVELS

EXPLORING THE DESIGN POSSIBILITIES inherent in levels presents a new challenge to the imagination and skill of the store architect. A shift in levels by a short flight of stairs has been used quite often in specialty shops and many types of retail stores to set off demonstration areas, accentuate departmental layout and highlight settings for special sales appeal. Now the true multi-level plan is becoming increasingly popular in all types of stores, including the suburban store and even the supermarket, which ordinarily is considered as a one-

level operation. This trend toward levels in suburban stores and shopping centers is encouraged by the need to increase parking space in relation to shopping area. Thus, multi-level parking with direct entrances to various store levels is being introduced in some of the newer shopping centers.

Wallach's, below, is an outstanding example of multi-level design in which levels expand and segregate sales areas, yet also give a feeling of overall unity and allow the customer to see all the merchandise in the store.

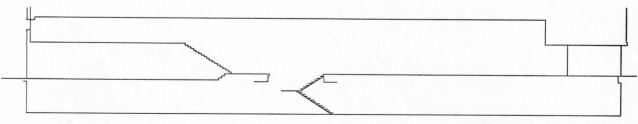

Wallach's, Jamaica, N. Y.
Ketchum, Giná & Sharp, Architects

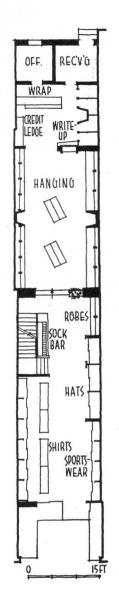

DESIGN EMPHASIS ON LEVELS

George & Lester's, Racine, Wis.
Morris Lapidus, Architect

THE DESIGN of the store front dramatizes both levels. The staircase, which leads to fitting rooms and space for future expansion, instead of being unobtrusive, is a dominant feature of the interior. The suit department in the rear of the store is raised slightly and a soffit is introduced to create a clearcut space division and a more intimate sales atmosphere. A fireplace and controlled lighting in this area heighten the personal effect desired by the owner.

Hedrich-Blessing

Tom Ballenger

d store fixtures and display

"FIXTURES are designed solely to display and sell consumer goods. They are a part of whatever atmosphere the architect is endeavoring to create and should never overpower the customer. Fixtures should be integrated as well as possible with the structure and lighting. In fact, the fixture work often *is* the store architecture and should be as unobtrusive as good architecture."

Daniel Laitin

"... and 'What is the best possible fixture design for any specific purpose?' The answer is, 'No fixtures at all.' In other words, the ideal is to maintain merchandise at the proper levels for inspection and handling without the aid of the present opaque, perishable and expensive fixturing methods. Most designers are now working toward that goal and doing everything possible to eliminate the bulkiness and insistent appearance of their fixtures."

Daniel Schwartzman

Victor Loczi

**Record Shop, Pittsburgh, Pa.
John Schurko, Architect**

Hugh Stern

WHOLESALE DISPLAY—SALES ROOM

Cobblers of California, New York, N. Y.
Gerhard E. Karplus, Architect

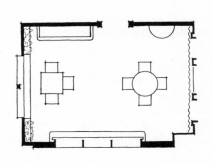

THE PROBLEM HERE is simple, quick-to-grasp display of the entire available stock in cases where it is accessible for examination by the buyers. This scheme is also adaptable for retail shoe display and sales in a limited area in a small store.

FITTING

STOCK

SALES

0   15 FT.

Dana Festive Fashions, New York, N. Y.
Ketch'um, Giná & Sharp, Architects

Focal point in this Madison Avenue dress shop is the casual, easily changed display area. Background colors are neutral to show off merchandise

Salvatore C. Valastro

store fixtures and display

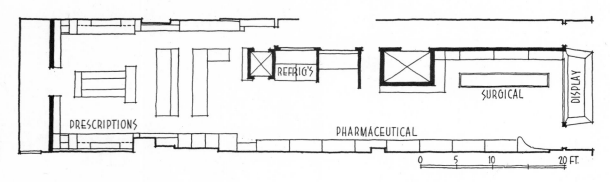

**William Radoff Pharmacy,
New York, N. Y.
Seymour R. Joseph, Architect**

In an ethical pharmacy, design is much more functional, unadorned and; in this case, handsome. Flexibility in its usual sense is not important. The result is a logical plan, cleancut handling of fixtures, especially in the prescription department (below left). Drawers and display cases are tailored to fit special items of fairly constant stock.

Ben Schnall

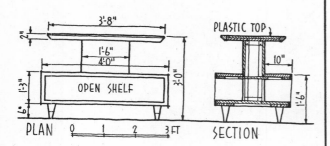

PLAN   0 1 2 3 FT   SECTION

**Dorothea Pharmacy, Mt. Vernon, N. Y.
Daniel Laitin, Architect**

*Above: Detail of center island counters
for sundry impulse-buying items. Below:
Detail of cosmetic unit with lift-up mirror
located in serpentine counter at left of
photograph*

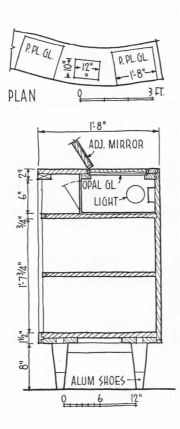

Julius Shulman

**Bercu's Tobacco Shop, Los Angeles, Calif.
Welton Becket and Associates,
Architect**

*Custom fixtures for smoker's needs include walk-in glass humidor
for imported cigars and counters for cigars, cigarettes, candy,
dry drugs, magazines and liquor*

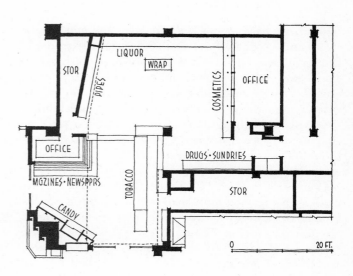

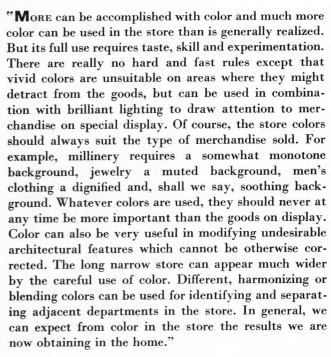

Tom Ballenger

e color

"MORE can be accomplished with color and much more color can be used in the store than is generally realized. But its full use requires taste, skill and experimentation. There are really no hard and fast rules except that vivid colors are unsuitable on areas where they might detract from the goods, but can be used in combination with brilliant lighting to draw attention to merchandise on special display. Of course, the store colors should always suit the type of merchandise sold. For example, millinery requires a somewhat monotone background, jewelry a muted background, men's clothing a dignified and, shall we say, soothing background. Whatever colors are used, they should never at any time be more important than the goods on display. Color can also be very useful in modifying undesirable architectural features which cannot be otherwise corrected. The long narrow store can appear much wider by the careful use of color. Different, harmonizing or blending colors can be used for identifying and separating adjacent departments in the store. In general, we can expect from color in the store the results we are now obtaining in the home."

José A. Fernandez

Oppenheim Collins, Huntington, N. Y.
Adolph Novak, Architect

Ben Schnall

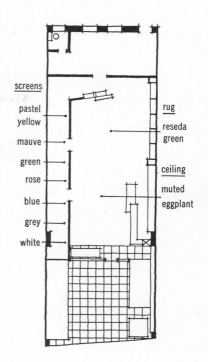

Screens, painted seven harmonizing colors and supported by
floor-to-ceiling black metal rods, partially hide stock

TWO COLOR SCHEMES FOR STORES

Above: Golub's Shoe Store, Bronx, N. Y.

Below: Mary Elizabeth Shop, Pelham, N. Y.

José A. Fernandez, Architect

WARM colors are used in entrance to store below, cool
ones in interior as non-distracting background for
stock. Street door and ceiling of front display area are
of mahogany, sign is dark green, floor is green terrazzo,
long display shelf and other small ones are hung from
poles of four different colors. Inside, floor is gray and
dark green, checkerboard walls and wood moldings are
off-white, horizontal-grain panels are blue-gray, directional signs are dark blue-green.

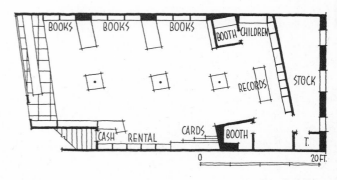

Gottscho-Schleisner

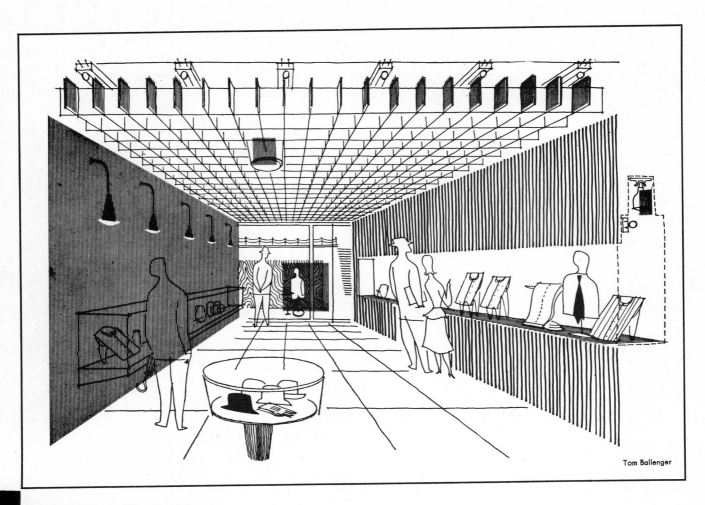

Tom Ballenger

f store lighting

"STORES in the past few years have stepped up their general lighting level to five or six times the prewar intensities. This shows that they are aware of the selling power of light. But, in using this new selling tool, they have created a sea of light which is also a sea of monotony. What is lacking is not the engineering know-how, but the taste and skill of the designer. Lighting, like any other creative effort, must be interesting. To achieve this, it must be used with due consideration to contrast, perspective and color as well as foot candle power. In other words, there must be design as well as engineering."

Abe Feder
Lighting Consultant

Sign is of aluminum with concealed white fluorescent tubing which reflects on polished granite surface to give striking effect. Arcade type front continues lighting design of interior. Note ceiling illumination glass panels, set flush, and use of incandescent spots

Ansonia Shoes, Philadelphia, Pa.
José A. Fernandez, Architect
Ballinger Co., Associated Architects

Dabby Shop, New York, N. Y.
Seymour Joseph, Architect

Ben Schnall

Above: Pelham Pharmacy, Pelham, N. Y. Joseph and Vladeck, Architects. Below: Photo Art Shop, Trenton, N. J. José A. Fernandez, Architect

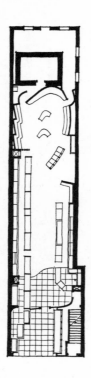

Directional lighting through incandescent spots over counter, also gooseneck reflectors over picture display on right wall and over book display case

Cargoes, Inc. (above) is interesting contrast in lighting approach, with single spotlighted letter as only identifying sign on this stage-set type of store without conventional display

Above: Detail of interior lighting of Photo Art Shop. Note neat appearance of fixtures

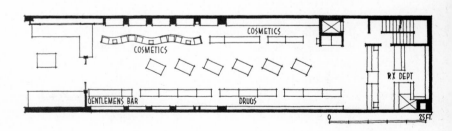

Dorothea Pharmacy, Mount Vernon, N.Y. Daniel Laitin, Architect. Plan above of general layout indicates diverse lighting problems of pharmacy with much display and many types of lighting

Tom Ballenger

g storage

"STORAGE can be broken down into three classifications — (1) direct selling storage, (2) forward storage, which would include stock rooms directly back of the selling fixtures and perimeter stock areas, and (3) bulk and general storage, which would include the balance of all merchandise necessary to store operation in general. The bulk storage should be adjacent to receiving and marking areas and directly connected to selling departments; it should also be provided with adequate vertical transportation whenever necessary."

Alvin L. Weidt

DIRECT selling storage includes both *exposed* stock in showcases, on countertops, in open shelving or hanging on racks, and *concealed* stock in showcases, counters, drawers and behind cabinet doors. Some of the many techniques of combining these types of storage are shown in the following photographs, ranging from no storage at all, with the entire merchandise exposed for customer selection, to storage in hidden stock areas of all stock except that on display.

Dabby Shop, New York, N. Y.
Seymour R. Joseph, Architect

1

2

1. Spear's, Pittsburgh, Pa.; John Schurko, Designer
2. Foreman and Clark, Los Angeles, Calif.; Welton Becket and Associates, Architects
3. Corsetorium, New York, N. Y.; José A. Fernandez, Architect
4. Bercu Tobacco Shop, Los Angeles, Calif.; Welton Becket and Associates, Architects
5. Armstrong's, Cedar Rapids, Iowa; Alvin L. Weidt, Architect

PHOTOGRAPHERS

1. Rembrandt Studios
2. Julius Shulman
3. Gottscho-Schleisner
4. Julius Shulman
5. Vern Thompson

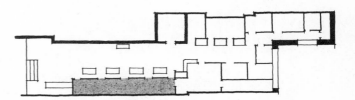

3

4

5

storage

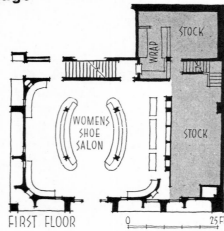

FIRST FLOOR 0   25 FT.

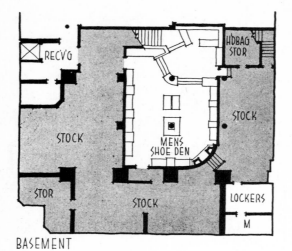

BASEMENT

Philip Fein

Salon type of layout where most merchandise is concealed: Frank Werner Co., San Francisco, Calif.; Hertzka and Knowles, Architects; Elizabeth Banning, Color Consultant; Dorothy Liebes, handwoven draperies

R. Wenkam

WAIKIKI BEACH SHOPS

Waikiki, Honolulu, Hawaii

Wimberly and Cook, Architects

COMPLETE SIMPLICITY in both plan and construction mark this new store building at Waikiki. When the project was started only two or three prospective tenants were interested, and maximum flexibility was called for to meet the needs of whatever tenants might eventually rent space. The site, on the grounds of the Royal Hawaiian Hotel, is 120 ft deep, with a 438-ft frontage on Kalakaua Avenue, one of Waikiki's main thoroughfares. Off-street parking was a must. Another requirement. stipulated in the property lease, was that the total height of the building be restricted to 30 ft.

To simplify financing, the building was designed as three identical units, each 136 ft long and 52 ft deep. which could be built one at a time, but which would look like one continuous structure when completed. The three units also made it easier to follow the slight curve in the street and the slight drop in sidewalk elevation.

Each unit consists of six 22 ft 8 in. bays, suitable for use either singly or in combination. Ceilings are high enough to permit installation of mezzanines if desired. Flexibility is further stressed in the basic structure — a simple flat slab resting on three rows of seven columns each. Front walls are glass from floor to ceiling, rear walls concrete block, plastered. Dividing partitions are metal lath and plaster. A parking lot runs the full length of the building at the rear, reached by two 10-ft passages between units.

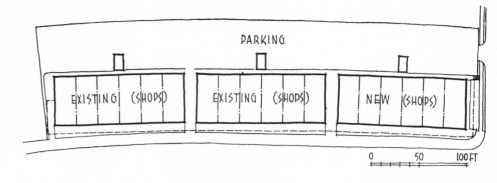

PARKING

EXISTING (SHOPS)   EXISTING (SHOPS)   NEW (SHOPS)

0   50   100 FT

WAIKIKI BEACH SHOPS

The three units are tied together chiefly by continuous concrete overhang. Tenants who leased space before building was finished had privilege of taking allowance for basic design to apply to cost of shop designed especially for their own requirements; McInerny's, in first building (above, right and opposite), had special front using a native sandstone

R. Wenkam

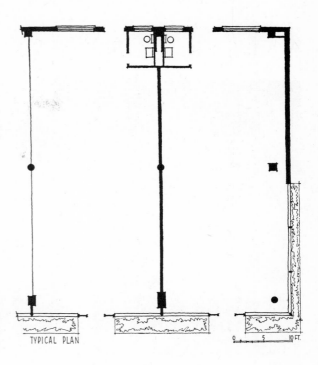

TYPICAL PLAN

0   5   10 FT.

Above: typical interior and corner shops. In latter, street half of end walls is glass from floor to ceiling, rear half is concrete block, plastered

WALTER N. BOYSEN CO. (HAWAII), LTD.

R. Wenkam Photo

Cyril W. Lemmon, Architect

Douglas Freeth, Associate

Lo & Katavolos, Engineers

Wilbert Choy's Makiki Nursery, Landscape Architects

THE Boysen Company's Honolulu building was planned not merely as a local outlet store, but as division headquarters for the Pacific trade. Provision had to be made, therefore, for easy space expansion as required. The solution was this one-story building consisting of five stores and a warehouse; three of the stores are "in reserve," and will be leased to other firms until such time as the owning company needs more space.

Ben Pang Photo

Foundation — Concrete piles

Framing — Reinforced concrete

Exterior walls — Sandstone

Interior walls — Plaster

Interior partitions — Hollow tile

Floors — Flagstone

Ceilings — Concrete

Sash — Steel

Store fronts — Bronze

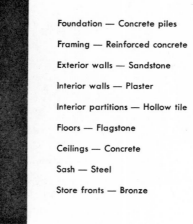

Billy Howell Photo

SEARS, ROEBUCK & CO., HONOLULU

Ben Pang Photos

Guy N. Rothwell, Architect

Edmund C. Abrams, Associate

IN appearance a two-story building, this Honolulu store has three selling levels and a total of about 200,000 ft of floor space. It was pushed a full story underground to keep it in scale with its contemporary neighbors.

Truck ramp and freight entrance are on the principal street front (left). Off-street parking areas can accommodate 500 cars.

Foundation — Reinforced concrete

Framing — Reinforced concrete

Exterior walls — Reinforced concrete, plastered

Interior walls — Plaster

Roof — 5-ply asphalt and felt

Floors — Reinforced concrete

Ceilings — Metal lath and plaster

Roger Sturtevant

NEW CHAPTER IN STORES STORY

JOSEPH MAGNIN STORE IN STONESTOWN

Branch Store for Joseph Magnin
Stonestown, San Francisco

Welton Becket and Associates
  Architects

L. F. Robinson
  Structural Engineer

Deane & Hill
  Mechanical Engineers

DESIGN OF LUXURY STORES and shopping centers by the Welton Becket office has come to be a modern success story. This Joseph Magnin store is the latest of a group that includes Bullock's Pasadena, Bullock's Westwood, in southern California, Stonestown Shopping Center, and Hillsdale and Stanford shopping centers. This latest product inevitably takes on the added significance of considerable momentum in store design and decorating. Incidentally, the architectural group executed the interior design and decor including all furnishings, fixtures and appointments from ash stands to monogrammed wallpaper.

The building, of reinforced concrete with exterior facing of Travertine, consists of a main floor, basement and mezzanine. All merchandise deliveries are made through a tunnel which terminates at a truck loading dock adjacent to the store's basement.

One of the interesting features is the dual-purpose display and selling rooms, of which there are four. During the selling hours these rooms serve as sales and fitting rooms; in the evening a series of sliding doors converts them into sidewalk display rooms.

While the building is contemporary in concept and expression, there is no dedicated dogma in it. One of the display-selling rooms, for example, is done in "fantastic Victorian," another in "Louis XVI." Interiors throughout the store exhibit wide variety of styling and a good deal of glamorized grandeur, all carefully calculated to capture feminine interest and to arouse that never-underestimated power of a woman.

Sidewalk frontage is used for display purposes only at night. In store hours the spaces are curtained off for sales rooms

Lower walls are of Travertine marble; upper walls in painted concrete with wide grooves delineating a modular pattern

JOSEPH MAGNIN STORE

Roger Sturtevant

Large entrance canopy gives store identification in the shopping center without the usual huge sign. On the wall facing parking lot the sign is also restrained but still has sufficient prominence on the sheer wall

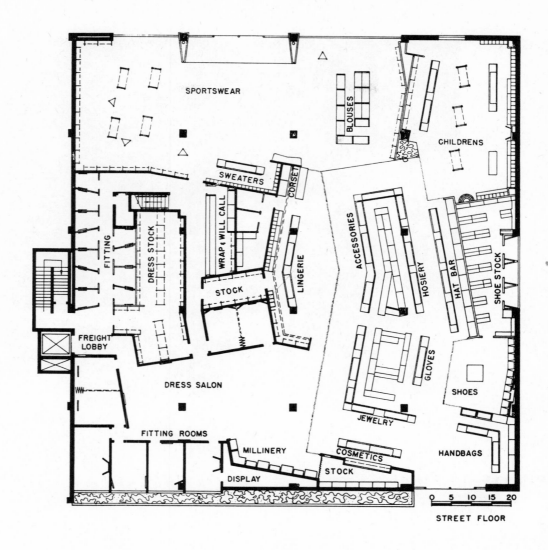

STREET FLOOR

0 5 10 15 20

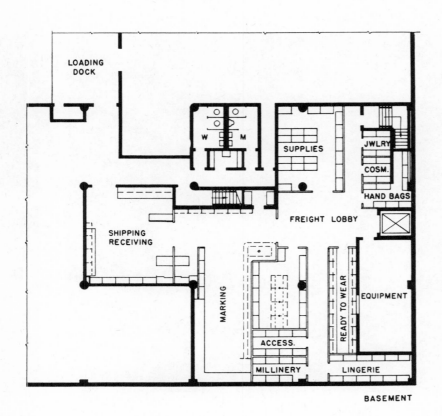

BASEMENT

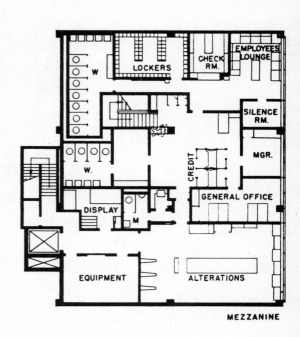

MEZZANINE

JOSEPH MAGNIN STORE

Roger Sturtevant

40

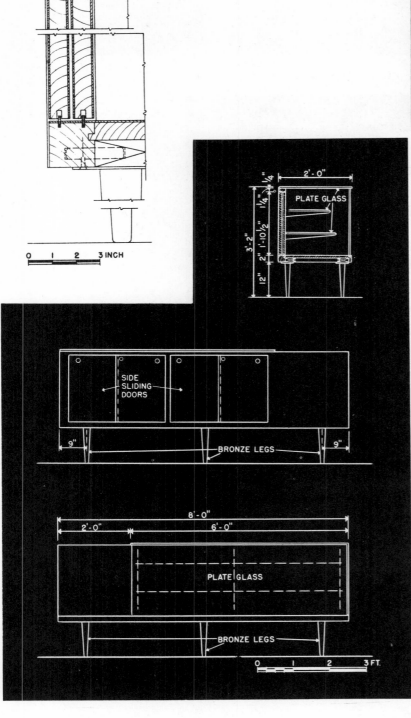

PLATE GLASS

2'-0"

3'-2"

SIDE SLIDING DOORS

9"   BRONZE LEGS   9"

8'-0"

2'-0"   6'-0"

PLATE GLASS

BRONZE LEGS

0 1 2 3 INCH

0 1 2 3 FT.

Cosmetics department (above) uses typical open-end showcase detailed at left, also recessed wall case. Mural above case is done in cast fragments in entarsia and scraffitto, by Mary Bowling. Hat bar (top of opposite page) is just about the longest straight line in the store. This and view below it show typical lighting, also the pattern of terrazzo floor

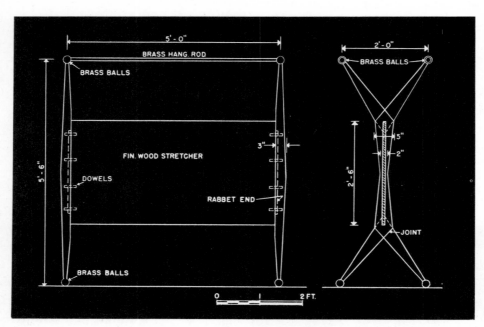

BRASS HANG. ROD
5' - 0"
BRASS BALLS
FIN. WOOD STRETCHER
5' - 6"
3"
DOWELS
RABBET END
BRASS BALLS
0   1   2 FT.

2' - 0"
BRASS BALLS
5"
2"
2' - 6"
JOINT

Sportswear (opposite page, top) is largest area, has Danish cork floors and specially designed hanging racks, shown in details. Children's section (bottom of opposite page) uses smaller version of this rack, has carpeting of honey colored wool grospoint. Note, in background, Victorian bear hat rack for window display

JOSEPH MAGNIN STORE

Roger Sturtevant

This page, top corner: booths in credit department on mezzanine floor. Above: main entrance doors are of glass in aluminum frames. Interior walls in plaster, wood or cork, in various colors in different departments. Right: carpeted flooring helps to delineate sections

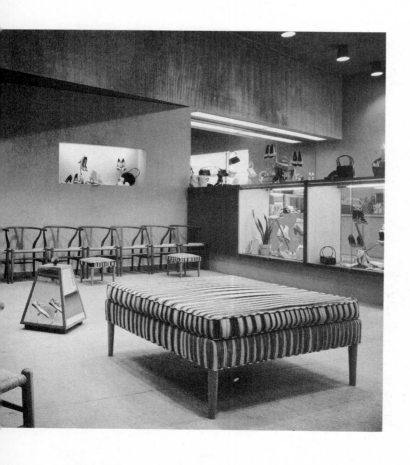

Dress salon (above) has wallpaper designed by the architects with JM monogram pattern, in gray on tan, or tan on gray. Chairs are Italian, covered with thaibok silks from Siam. Love seats have Indian silk tweed covering. Shoe department (left) has Danish oak chairs, hassocks covered with striped fabric designed by the architects

Shown here are the dual-purpose display and fitting rooms — display windows at night, sales rooms by day. Here the architects pulled out the stylistic stops. One (right) is modern, with blue glass cloth wall covering, plastic table, collage on wall. The one at the bottom of the page is called fantastic Victorian, and George Wright, designer in charge, had fun in the antique shops picking up the wicker furniture and the whatnot. Another fun-and-games item is the Cupid chandelier. Sofa here, as in the other of the four rooms, is in thaibok silk

Roger Sturtevant

JOSEPH MAGNIN STORE

GARDEN CITY BRANCH

Frank Majer, Architect

THIS STORE, finished in the spring of 1952, is the first suburban branch for Martin's of Brooklyn, a department store. In planning, the architect carefully located and articulated the various departments in relation to pedestrian traffic flow, so that men seeking their department will not have to pass through a women's department, and vice versa. In general, young people's and sportswear, as well as impulse items such as gloves, jewelry, etc. are located at street level, while the higher priced dresses and gift shop are located on the second floor. The architect designed all interiors, including merchandising fixtures and lighting.

FOR MARTIN'S

Morris Lapidus,
Associate Architect and
Interior Designer
McKim, Mead and White,
Supervising Architects

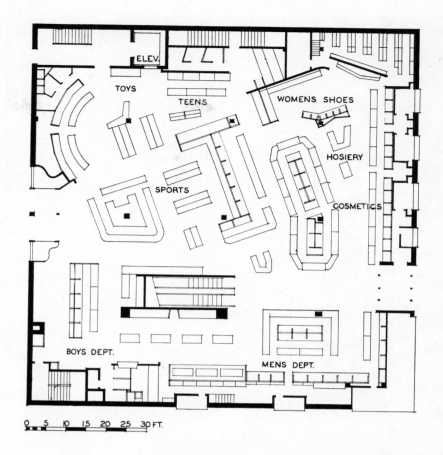

Gottscho-Schleisner

BULLOCK'S WESTWOOD—A NEW SUBURBAN STORE

Welton Becket & Associates, Architects & Engineers
Murray Erick Associates, Structural Engineers
Hillburg, Byler & Hengstler, Mechanical Engineers
Robert Herrick Carter, Landscape Architect

LOCATED IN WESTWOOD VILLAGE, in suburban Los Angeles, this department store with restaurant on its top floor is especially interesting for its 3-level arrangement of parking and access. By closely correlating garaging and retailing, the architect has achieved a scheme that permits the customer to park his car only a few yards from and at the same level as the section he is visiting. Total parking space will handle 1000 cars.

The design capitalizes on the natural slope of the 4-acre site by providing two principal merchandising levels, each with its pedestrian entrance directly from the street, as well as making possible parking at each level. Six entrances enable the shopper to reach his destination in the shortest possible time, whether he arrives on foot or by car.

Working closely with Raymond Dexter, Bullock's planning director, the architect completely designed the interior, including dress labels and wrapping paper.

Douglas M. Simmonds

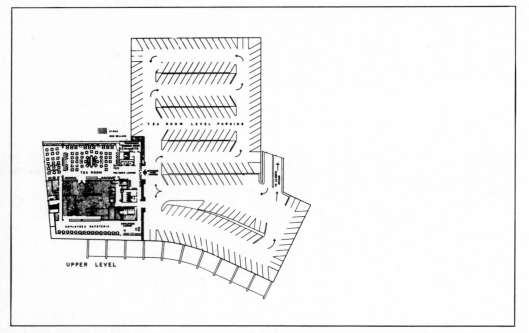

UPPER LEVEL

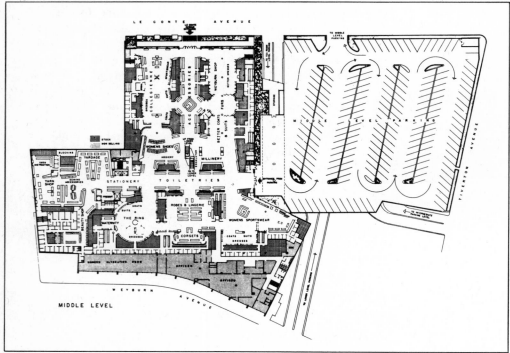

MIDDLE LEVEL

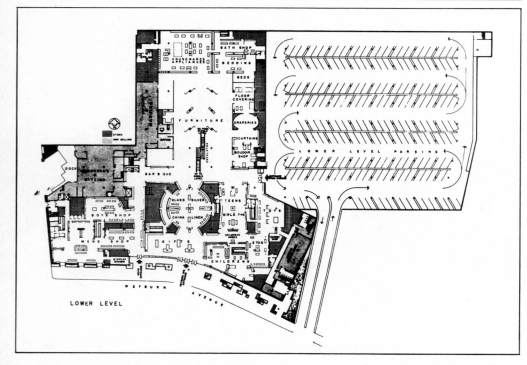

LOWER LEVEL

Douglas M. Simmonds

The three plans at left show how the three levels are articulated for both pedestrians and cars. Photo at left, above, shows top floor, which houses the restaurant. Middle level ramp entrance from the street is shown above, right. In the photo of the entrance detail at right, note the oversized faience tile which was designed by the architect for this job and used on several of the building's elevations

Douglas M. Simmonds

Several materials are used for the exterior walls: concrete painted pale green, Arizona mint stone, fieldstone, and architect designed large size faience tile. The extensive use of tropical planting emphasizes the California character of the store's appearance

Ben Schnall

LANE BRYANT—BROOKLYN

Sanders-Malsin-Reiman, Architects

John W. Harris Associates, General Contractor

CHIEF PROBLEM of the architects in converting this L-shaped building for Lane Bryant was the luring of customers from the main entrance to the main sales area. The building occupies a corner site with the long arm of the L stretching back from the entrance as a narrow corridor leading to the elevators and upper floors (plans, page 56).

The building is a very old one, formerly used for fur storage. The exterior was left unchanged except for new show windows and stainless steel spandrel panels and signs which were fastened directly over the existing cast iron spandrels. The corner was opened up so that the show windows would be clearly visible from both streets at the intersection. The three lower floors were

remodeled for sales usage, the fourth floor was converted to offices and a beauty parlor, and the balance of the building was left for fur storage and mechanical equipment.

On the ground floor the long Smith Street wing was given over to counter sales and made a frank corridor toward the rear sales area. Since traffic here is heavy, the teak plank floor is rather surprising; brushed nightly with a sealer, it is bearing up very well, the owners report, and is proving well worth the cost (twice that of terrazzo) because of the warmth of its appearance.

Despite a difference in ground level, there are no stairs on the main floor of the Smith Street wing. The entire wing is a continuous ramp from the entrance to

the elevators. At the end of the "corridor" a stylized arrow on the wall discreetly points the way to the right toward the main sales area. Fluorescent-lighted teak railings line the several steps at the wing-junction, again leading the customer on toward the more important areas of the store. Elevators, also at the junction, have been placed to open out toward the main areas.

The poor condition of the existing walls precluded the use of plaster and made a dry type of construction economical. Patented steel struts and connectors, fastened to the walls, serve as dividers for perforated asbestos cement wall panels, and as standards for the specially designed knife brackets which hold shelving and hang rods. The standards were designed for complete flexibility, all brackets being adjustable and interchangeable; the shelves can be rearranged overnight if required by seasonal selling demands.

Strong rich colors are used in all sales areas. Chandeliers, racks and special display cases were designed by the architects; cabinets are walnut, paneled walls are birch.

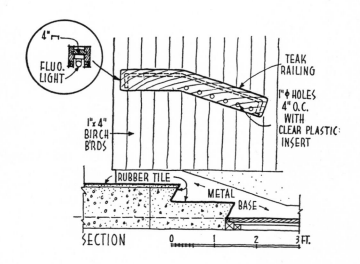

Ben Schnall

The long corridor leading from main entrance (far left, opposite page). to main sales area (below) has show windows along one whole side; over the windows is a combination curtain track and light cove

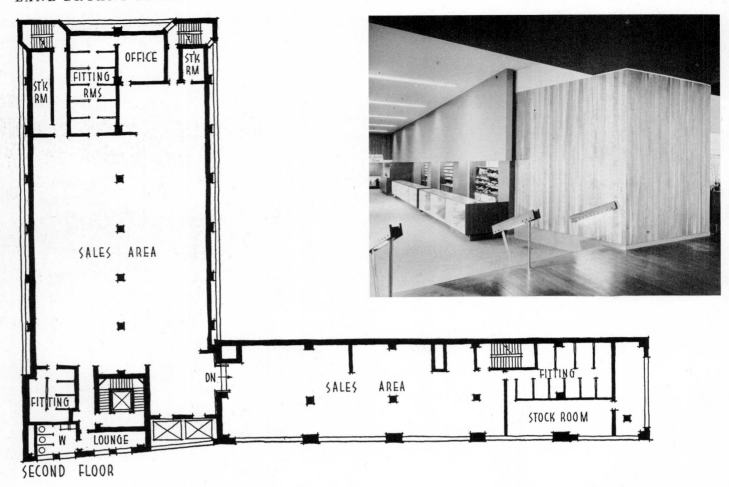

SECOND FLOOR

STK RM

FITTING RMS

OFFICE

STK RM

SALES AREA

FITTING

W

LOUNGE

DN

SALES AREA

FITTING

STOCK ROOM

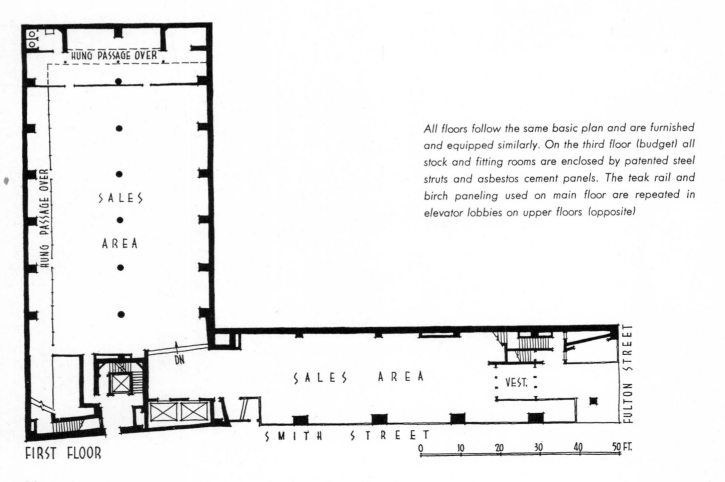

All floors follow the same basic plan and are furnished and equipped similarly. On the third floor (budget) all stock and fitting rooms are enclosed by patented steel struts and asbestos cement panels. The teak rail and birch paneling used on main floor are repeated in elevator lobbies on upper floors (opposite)

FIRST FLOOR

HUNG PASSAGE OVER

HUNG PASSAGE OVER

SALES AREA

DN

SALES AREA

VEST.

FULTON STREET

SMITH STREET

0   10   20   30   40   50 FT.

LANE BRYANT STORE

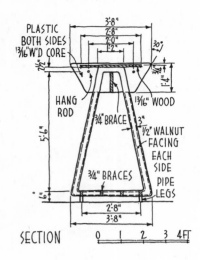

PLASTIC BOTH SIDES
$\frac{13}{16}$" W'D CORE

3'-8"
2'-8"
2'-0"
1'-2"
30°
$\frac{3}{4}$"
1'-4"
$2\frac{1}{2}$"

HANG ROD

$\frac{3}{4}$" BRACE

$\frac{13}{16}$" WOOD

3"

$\frac{1}{2}$" WALNUT FACING EACH SIDE

$\frac{3}{4}$" BRACES

PIPE LEGS

5'-6"

6"

2'-8"
3'-8"

SECTION   0 1 2 3 4 FT

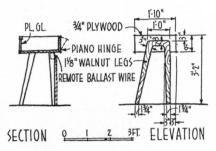

PL. GL.

$\frac{3}{4}$" PLYWOOD

1'-10"
1'-0"

PIANO HINGE

$1\frac{1}{8}$" WALNUT LEGS

REMOTE BALLAST WIRE

3"
3"
6"
3'-2"

$1\frac{3}{4}$" $1\frac{3}{4}$"
3'-3"

SECTION   0 1 2 3 FT   ELEVATION

Ben Schnall

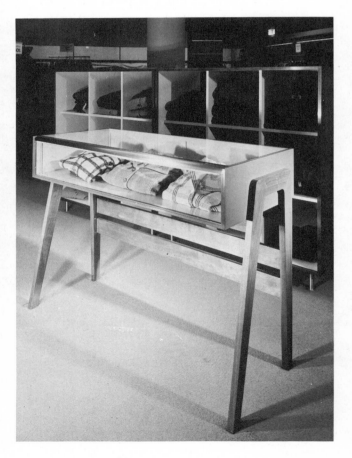

Above: air conditioning ducts are supported by patented steel struts and screened with perforated asbestos cement panels; panels are yellow, vents are bright red. Right: the architects designed dress and skirt racks and display cases

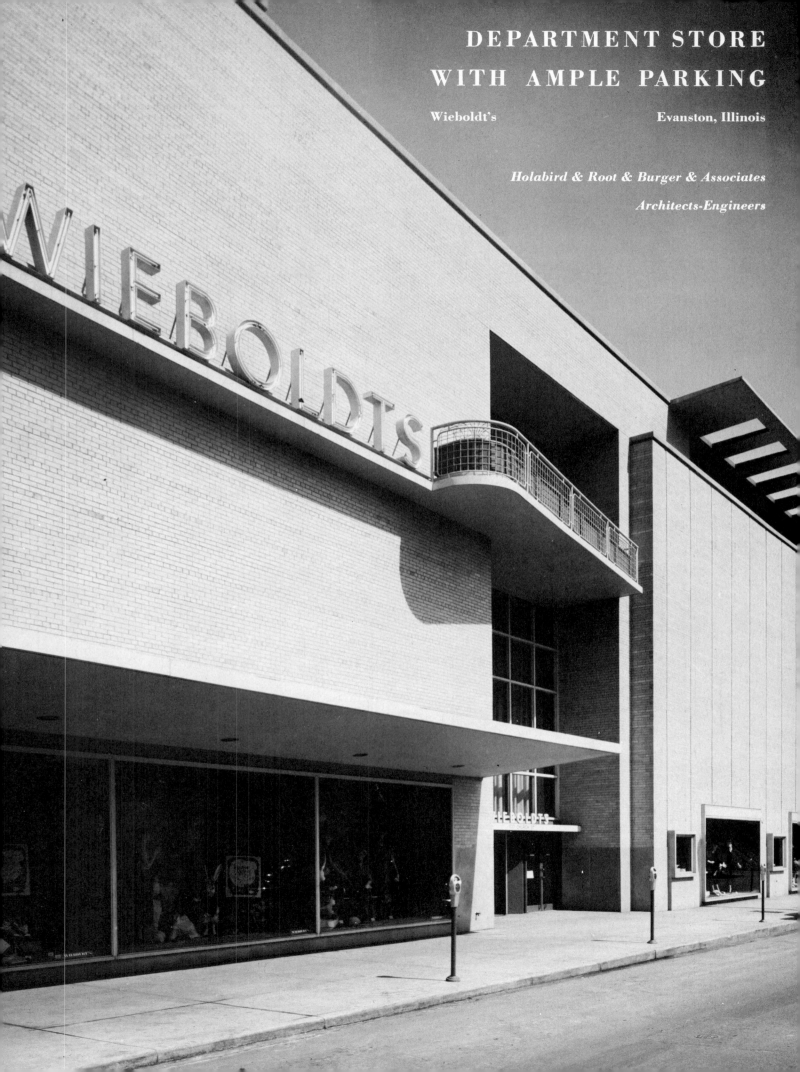

DEPARTMENT STORE
WITH AMPLE PARKING

Wieboldt's   Evanston, Illinois

Holabird & Root & Burger & Associates
Architects-Engineers

NORTH

RAILROAD

STORE BUILDING

STREET

STREET

Bridge

PARKING BUILDING

STREET

STREET

ALLEY

STREET

0   50   100   200

WIEBOLDT'S STORE

This newest structure in Wieboldt's chain of six department stores, all in the Chicago metropolitan area, incorporates many ideas proved in the owners' long merchandising experience; their first store opened in 1883, the Evanston branch in 1929. The new building is deliberately horizontal because Wieboldt's believes women prefer to shop as much as possible on one floor rather than several. The large site facilitates such a scheme. On each of the three floors above grade (and self-service basement) related departments are planned to be contiguous. There are virtually no windows in sales areas. The bays, relatively small, are sized to accommodate a flexible merchandising fixture layout (for which H. Allan Majestic & Assoc. were consultants) and for economy in the reinforced concrete construction

Dn

Up

FRT

FOOD MART

SERVICE CORR.

REF'S

Escalator

Coal Manholes

RCVG OFF.

Dn

Chute

PACKING & SHIPPING

REF.

BAKERY

REF.

KITCHEN

DISH WASH.

SODA LUNCHEONETTE

W.

M

SERVICE & CHECK

Up

Dn

M

Photo preceding page
by Hedrich-Blessing

RESTAURANT

VEST.

Dn   Up

FIRST FLOOR

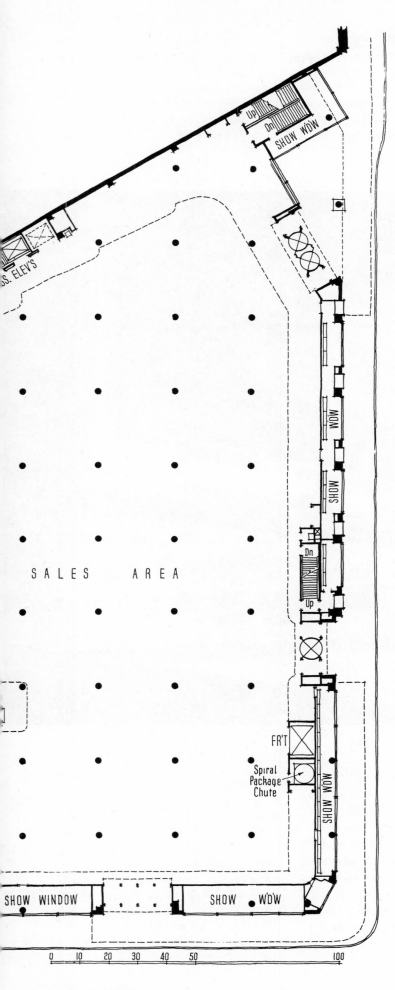

SHOW W'DW

SS. ELEV'S

SALES   AREA

SHOW   W'DW

FR'T

Spiral
Package
Chute

SHOW WINDOW   SHOW · W'DW

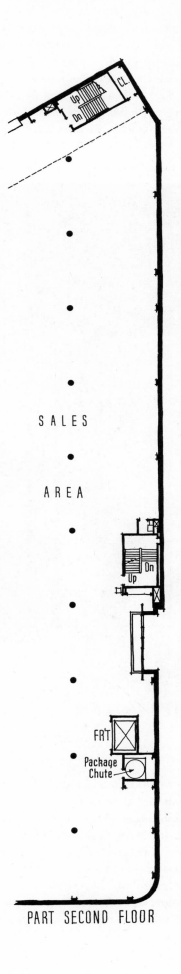

CL.

SALES

AREA

FR'T

Package
Chute

PART SECOND FLOOR

WIEBOLDT'S DEPARTMENT STORE

Among the store's many up-to-date ideas is a package-gathering system using chutes and belt conveyors to simplify the problem of getting to one place all the purchases made by each customer. It also speeds delivery service. From the point of purchase wrapped packages to be taken by the customer may be conveyed to a first-floor service desk or to either deck of the parking building; packages for delivery go to the basement and onto delivery trucks, without handling, within minutes after sale.

One of the main problems in downtown Evanston, as elsewhere, is parking; hence the huge parking structure which accommodates 744 cars on two floors. Its top deck was opened for public use some months before the store itself was ready

Because windows don't admit enough light to display merchandise well, and do admit dirt, they are virtually eliminated. Lighting is generally from louvered fluorescent fixtures, with incandescent fixtures for accents and special lighting. Each flush ceiling fixture is also an access panel to service lines in the furred space above; over each fixture is a pullbox with an extra electrical connection to accommodate future changes on the floor above or below. There are two heating systems: one for air conditioning during business hours; the other, radiation used to maintain 65 F temperature in off hours in winter. Automatic controls govern temperatures throughout.

Second-floor bridge, like garage and store which it connects, is reinforced concrete. At garage end of bridge is control tower from which an observer telephones attendant at street-level entrance directions for cars to be parked on second floor. First-floor cars are directed by an elaborate system of lights

Walls of the three-story building, virtually windowless, are relieved of monotony by pattern and texture of the face brick. Entrances are spacious, in keeping with Wieboldt's intention of providing friendly rather than frenzied service. Show windows and cases are provided along street facades and entrance shown below for both small objects and large

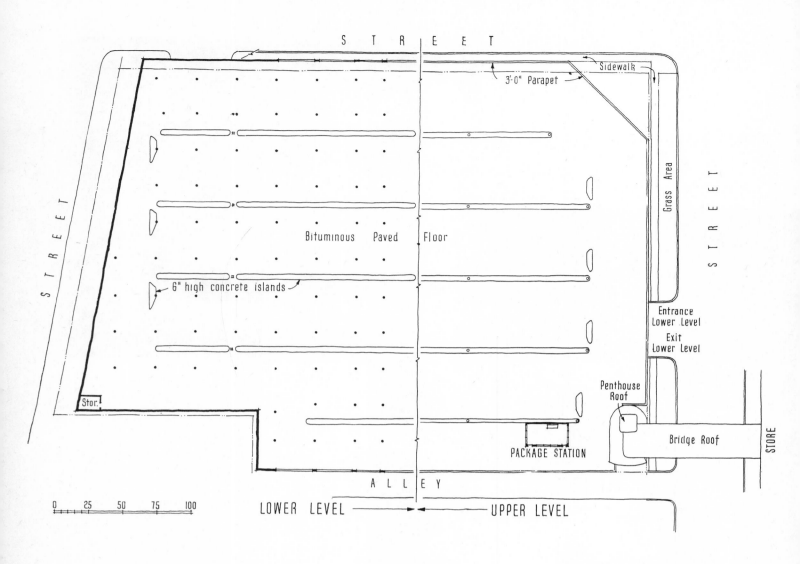

S T R E E T

Sidewalk

3'-0" Parapet

S T R E E T

Grass Area

S T R E E T

Bituminous Paved Floor

6" high concrete islands

Entrance
Lower Level

Exit
Lower Level

Penthouse
Roof

Stor.

Bridge Roof

STORE

PACKAGE STATION

A L L E Y

| 0 | 25 | 50 | 75 | 100 |

LOWER LEVEL ◄───►── UPPER LEVEL

WIEBOLDT'S DEPARTMENT STORE

Hedrich-Blessing Studio Photos

Plan of parking building, above, shows lower level at left, upper level at right. Customer driving in at lower level is directed to available parking space, crosses bridge to store Customer leaving store crosses bridge, picks up packages at station on level where her car is parked. In photo of store interior, right, note simplicity of fixtures and interior treatment; nothing in sales areas is permitted to compete with the merchandise

AN ART STORE DESIGNED FOR MODERN MERCHANDISING

Kassel S. Slobodien Photos

Arthur Brown & Bro., Inc., New York City   **Thomas Sapolsky, A.I.A., and Kassel S. Slobodien, Architects**

IN these days of streamlined selling, most artist supply stores paradoxically have remained disorganized and cluttered-up merchandising areas. Store owners, it would seem, have been convinced that purchase impulse is induced into the artistic soul by a happy abandon of disarranged paints and pads, scattered easels and drawing instruments.

Note that display window spot-lights form an integral part of egg-crate louvered ceiling. Right: section through show window indicates plenum chamber. Fan runs continuously in summer to relieve air-conditioning system, periodically in winter to eliminate condensation

Moldings with lugs to fit perforated backing give adjustable book support

Architects Sapolsky and Slobodien have broken this tradition dramatically and conclusively in the design of the Arthur Brown & Bro. store. An "open front" design of unusual visual impact has been developed by the use of a continuous display window which, in combination with an entrance vestibule which has wide entrance doors of tempered plate glass, stretches from one end of the 65-ft. front to the other. The planning of this display-entrance element is given added unity of design and purpose by the egg-crate louvered ceiling, used for illumination, which extends continuously over the whole area. The show window is exposed to a minimum

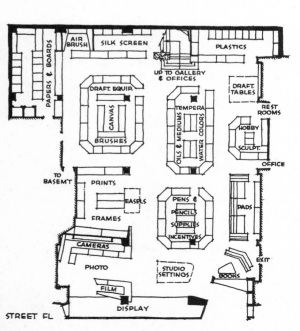

The wide show window and entrance is framed on the facade by cedar colored marble. Projecting marble wings at both ends of the display front are pierced by see-through show cases which can be viewed from either side. The photography department and book center, both facing the open window, were designed both as display backgrounds and as partial screens for departments behind. The book center uses a perforated asbestos display board. The photography screen is a patterned plywood painted bright coral. Columns flanking the entrance doors are covered with fluted fireproof oak panels painted deep blue. Interior wall and ceiling colors are warm gray and yellow with accents of blue and coral. Fixtures are of light oak

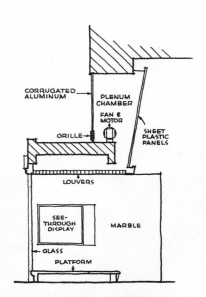

SECTION THROUGH SHOW WINDOW

Labels in diagram:
CORRUGATED ALUMINUM
PLENUM CHAMBER
FAN & MOTOR
SHEET PLASTIC PANELS
GRILLE
LOUVERS
SEE-THROUGH DISPLAY
MARBLE
GLASS
PLATFORM

PHOTOGRAPHY DEPARTMENT

amount of veiling glare as the facade faces north and is surrounded by tall buildings.

The many items which the store offers have been departmentalized into retail sales sections in accordance with accepted modern merchandising practices. A modular fixture system consisting of two types of counter units for display and storage and one type of back fixture with adjustable shelves allows complete flexibility for the rearrangement of departments.

The store is completely air conditioned. Stairs at the rear lead to reception areas, offices and an exhibition gallery on the mezzanine. Basement is used for stock.

FILM COUNTER

BOOKS

Jonn Eken Dinwiddie A.I.A., Architect, and Richard Maxwell

LUXURY SHOP PRODUCED

LOCATED in an expensive shopping area and offering luxury items of imported silver, porcelain and bronze, this store has had to achieve its quiet elegance and good taste at a minimum of expense. The owners had plenty of resources in Copenhagen but few American dollars. Money for construction was necessarily rigidly restricted.

The architects thus solved this typical jewelry store problem on a basis of effective color and simple well-proportioned form. It's of note that the small display units on the exterior have no expensive frames. Surrounding moldings are simple, refined, and match the color of the wall. The one vivid accent is the fluted chromium column at the entrance.

The interior is suitably but modestly designed for the general display of many small expensive items. Special features such as the flatware sales cabinet, which is illustrated, have been created to assist the customer in a.

WITH A MINIMUM BUDGET

Roger Sturtevant Photos

S. Christian of Copenhagen, Inc.

San Francisco, Calif.

comfortable and orderly examination of merchandise. Dark mahogany was chosen for cabinet work as the best background for the gleaming silver and porcelain on display. The ceiling is a royal blue and other colors are in harmony to produce the desired luxury atmosphere. General lighting is provided by simple spots through diffusing lenses. The use of planting on both the exterior and interior adds life and color.

New Warsaw Bakery

Brooklyn, N. Y.

A MODERN OPEN FRONT BAKE SHOP

SINCE grandmother's day bakeries have been attract-ing passers-by with the pleasurable aromas of oven-fresh delicacies. Present day moppets (and grownups) are now not only subjected to this same sweet persuasion through the olfactory nerves but more and more frequently are faced with a formidable visual appeal as well. The combination is well-nigh irresistible, and per-haps in no other use is the "open front" so successful as in modern bakery design.

Architects Kaplan and Neivert have planned their shop with as open a front as possible. The three existing cast iron columns have been covered with aluminum; two of these columns, converted into pylons, support a low all-glass air conditioned showcase at the sidewalk line. The whole front is framed with red marble at top, sides, below the showcase and at the return of the en-trance vestibule. The plate glass front is well recessed and thus less vulnerable to veiling glare.

The shop is neatly organized on the interior, mer-chandise is attractively displayed, and lighting is of high intensity from inconspicuous sources. The plan is di-vided into two selling areas, one area to the left of the entrance is for special orders; the other, for general bake goods, forms a long L to the right. Both sections have generous well protected display areas and both have wrap-up counter and cash register facing customers. A refrigerated counter for ice cream cakes and candies is set diagonally at the rear.

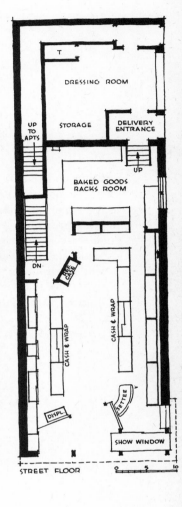

DRESSING ROOM

STORAGE

DELIVERY ENTRANCE

UP TO APTS

BAKED GOODS RACKS ROOM

UP

DN

CASH & WRAP

CASH & WRAP

DISPL.

SETTEE

SHOW WINDOW

STREET FLOOR

0   5   10

Alexandre Georges Photos

Robert Kaplan, A.I.A., and Marvin J. Neivert, Architects

The general lighting scheme is indirect augmented by direct recessed lensed units set into ceilings and coves. The wall fixture in the general bake goods section is worthy of note; it provides indirect lighting sources for the illumination of the built-in cove above and also, by the use of tilted plate glass shelves, clearly displays well-lighted merchandise against a luminous background.

Ceilings and walls above light coves are of soft lemon yellow. The under sides of light coves are green. The left side of the shop is painted red rouge color to match the marble of the entrance vestibule. The floor is light beige terrazzo. Natural wood counters and fixtures are of bleached oak.

HOW THE WELL-LIGHTED STORE SHOULD LOOK

Broadstreet's, Fifth Avenue, New York City

Kenneth C. Welch, A.I.A., Architect

THIS men's shop in the medium-price field goes all out to attractively display as much of its merchandise as possible. In doing so it incorporates the interior lighting principles set forth by its architect at a recent engineers' conference.*

Mr. Welch believes that a store should keep as simple a total environment as is compatible with the atmosphere desired. This is done first, by keeping the apparent brightness of the lighting equipment itself reduced to a

minimum (its effect should be seen but its appearance not heard). Second, by planning the interior so that the reflection factors and surface characteristics of the architectural and equipment surfaces will produce, when illuminated, brightnesses and brightness patterns that are simple in themselves. Mr. Welch assures us that conscientious use of these two principles will give merchandise full right of way.

The control of the directional distribution of light to best display the kind of merchandise being illuminated is also an important point. It is possible with good de-

* Conference of the Milwaukee Chapter of the Illuminating Engineering Society, May 19, 1949.

Section at right clearly indicates general lighting scheme. Fluorescent tubes behind metal grids are combined with spotlights for added illumination of merchandise appraisal areas. Also shown are lighting details of shirt fixtures (illustrated in photograph at left) and neckware display cases (illustrated upper right). Note the high quality of display lighting combined with low brightness of lighting equipment, simplicity of architectural surfaces and brightness patterns

sign, using the proper reflectors and lenses for control, to produce the highest brightness on fashion apparel or soft goods of diffuse texture. This attracts the customer and saves equipment and electrical energy as areas used for display of this kind are small. On the other hand, merchandise such as silverware, appliances and automobiles, with primarily specular surfaces, need an overhead or surrounding brightness pattern which does most to bring out their form. Low brightness incandescent or fluorescent lights, or both, surrounded or partly reflected to other architectural surfaces are obviously the best answer in these cases.

The use of a combination of fluorescent and incandescent light sources in even distribution to bring out correct color values is generally advisable. Incandescent alone accents the yellow and red colors; common fluorescent sources exaggerate the blues and purples.

Lastly, Mr. Welch emphasizes that the artificial lighting equipment used in a store must appear to be an integral part of the structure. This does not necessarily mean the use of special built-in equipment, but, preferably, simple, direct design with the use of mass-produced and packaged equipment.

The photographs and typical section of Broadstreet's illustrate how these simple but basically important lighting principles can be put to good merchandising use.

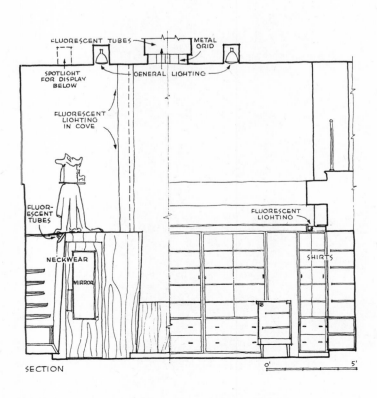

Ceiling is an off-white, walls are blended shades of gray, blue and warm tan. Carpet is rust colored. Fixtures are light oak

SHOE DEPARTMENT

SPORT COATS AND SLACKS

PAGING THE DISCRIMINATING TRAVELER

Shamrock Hotel Men's Shop, Houston, Texas

Brochstein's, Inc., Designers

CLOTHING

TOILETRIES   DISPLAY FOYER

THIS shop, in the words of the designers, has been "fashioned to attract the discriminating masculine trade which daily converges at the hotel, now a southern crossroads of the nation". Atmosphere, of the lush, clubby, substantial masculine variety, has been created here at considerable expense and with no holds barred to coax browsing customers into an expansive purchasing mood. Display is used for merchandising appeal also, but in a restricted, selective sense, subordinate to the overall atmosphere pattern.

The center of attraction of the well departmentalized store is the clothing section with its wall-carved mahogany mural which occupies a recess over the massive split-stone fireplace. The pomegranate red leather upholstered furniture, the cushioned settees, exotic woods, and end tables with specially designed lamps all convey an impression of comfort and elegance. Here in the privacy of well-appointed display rooms clients may also select woolens and fine linens for individual tailoring and shirting. Adjoining space provides fitting areas.

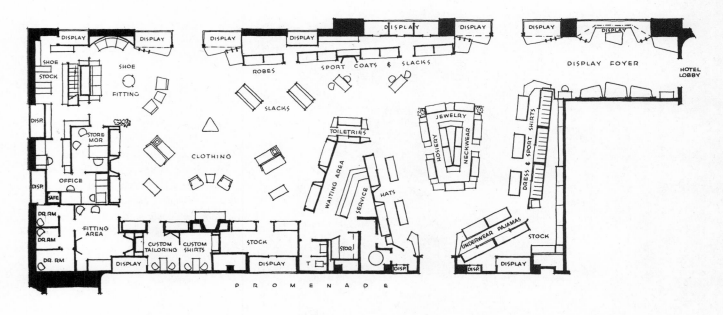

SHIRT DEPARTMENT

Elwood M. Payne Photos

This same decorative theme is carried all through the store, much of the merchandise being concealed in the interest of controlled atmosphere. Exceptions are the toiletries counter where display levels in the background are individually lighted and the wall fixtures in the shirt and hat departments where slots have been left in slid-ing doors so that customers may have a dignified peek at stock.

It is of interest to note in the illustrations of the shoe and the sportswear departments that the interior dis-plays are well integrated with window displays which face the streets.

HAT DEPARTMENT

The store fixtures are South American walnut. Furniture is upholstered in pome-granate colored leather. Carpeting is light gray; ceilings mocha. Potted plants have been used to add freshness and life to the setting. Handcarved mahogany plaques in background of the display foyer depict resources and progress of Houston

Harry H. Baskerville, Jr.

THE MOST NOTICEABLE fea-
ture of this new store
in the Statler Center is its
openness: each of its two
levels is a single large sales
area, departmentalized only
by the placement of display
cases and the use of color.
Show windows are continu-
ous and full-height on the
two street sides, with the
mezzanine cutting diagon-
ally across the rear of the
store between them. There
are two entrances (see plans,
page 79), one from the
street to the lower level,
and the other from the
hotel lobby to the mezzanine.

Eddy Harth, Statler Center

Los Angeles, California

OPEN PLAN FOR MENSWEAR STORE

Victor Gruen, Architect

R. L. Baumfeld, Associate in Charge

Harry H. Baskerville, Jr.

White ceilings and predomi-.
nantly white walls are enlivened
by frequent touches of bright
color. Open stairway to mezza-
nine is carpeted in lemon yel-
low; steel rail is finished in black

All fixtures and furniture were designed by architect. Show cases are birch, some with glass, others with lacquered panels in yellow, gray or white; all are raised from floor on brass legs to facilitate cleaning. Light fixtures are enameled in colors corresponding to the colors used on panels

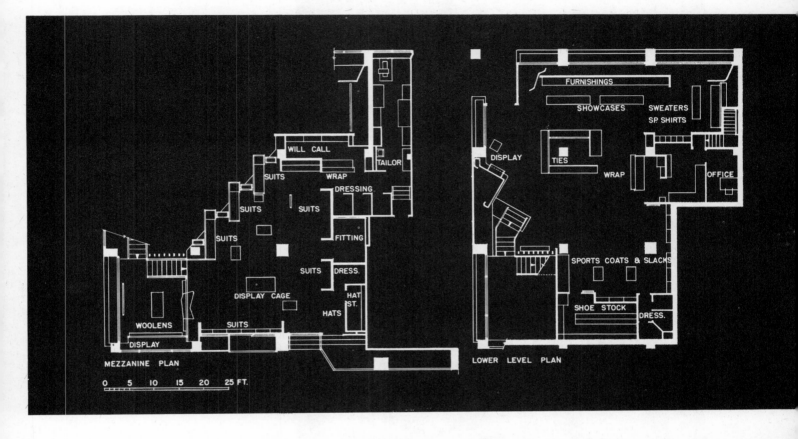

MEZZANINE PLAN

WILL CALL
TAILOR
SUITS WRAP
DRESSING
SUITS SUITS
SUITS FITTING
SUITS DRESS.
DISPLAY CAGE
HAT ST.
HATS
WOOLENS SUITS
DISPLAY

0 5 10 15 20 25 FT.

LOWER LEVEL PLAN

FURNISHINGS
SHOWCASES SWEATERS
SP. SHIRTS
DISPLAY TIES
WRAP OFFICE
SPORTS COATS & SLACKS
SHOE STOCK DRESS.

Floor covering on lower level is bold-patterned vinyl in blue, green, gray and white. Columns are gray, blue, yellow

Harry H. Baskerville, Jr.

Suit department occupies most of upper level. Hangrod cases are conventionally peripheral except for three low ones which, alternating with planting boxes, zig-zag across diagonal of mezzanine face at 45 deg angle. Main display case is large cage of silver-gray birch, prominently placed and well-mirrored; its horizontal members can be used for showing of ties and accessories. Carpeting is again lemon yellow, and color accents same as below

Julius Shulman Photos

STORE FOR THE BROWSING MUSIC LOVER

Gateway to Music, Inc., Los Angeles, Calif.

Rolf Sklarek, A.I.A., Architect

PARADISE for the music lover is this hospitable Los Angeles store where he may browse among books and albums and listen to records for as long as he likes. He even is treated to a welcoming cup of coffee when he enters!

Specializing in phonograph records (serious music only), with the emphasis on imported recordings from all over the world, the store also sells radios and tele-

vision sets. A book department operated by Brentano's rounds out the merchandise offered with books on music and art and music scores. The store has a well established clientele and does not depend on street traffic; it has a weekly radio program of recordings on a local station, supplemented by free record concerts monthly in its own quarters.

Requirements which the architect had to meet in

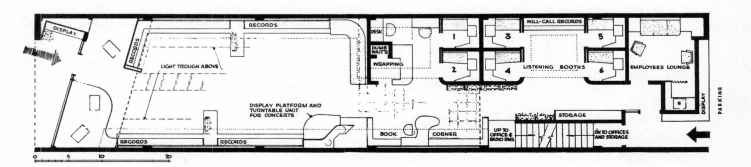

Julius Shulman Photos

For economy's sake all fixtures were made of soft wood and painted. Record shelves are lined with black battleship linoleum to prevent scuffing of albums. Strong colors are used throughout: light cove facias are red, egg-crate ceiling over rear portion is yellow, carpet green, walls are yellow, red and green

Records are lighted directly from concealed fluorescents in light cove above record shelves, general illumination is from concealed fluorescents in upper light trough. Spots in light trough are used for accent

remodeling the 20- by 100-ft. premises for the Gateway included considerable storage and shipping space for the import and export of records, and a large main sales floor open enough to provide space for the monthly concerts. The existing full basement and the mezzanine over the rear third of the store were used to good advantage in meeting those requirements — the former to house the offices, shipping and storage facilities, and the latter for the radio and television department, of only secondary merchandising importance. The whole ground floor was given to record and book sales, and the front section was kept completely open by the omission of sales counters. Patrons select their albums directly from the shelves, using a special shelf at approximately counter height for their tentative selections. The wrapping desk and the book corner are strategically located at about the center of the store, controlling both front and rear entrances. A concert platform containing dual turntables for the monthly concerts and display space for special radio cabinets is also used by visiting authors and musicians autographing books and records at parties (see photo at left, below).

**Robert K. Overstreet, Designer
for N. W. Overstreet, Assoc.
Architects & Engineers**

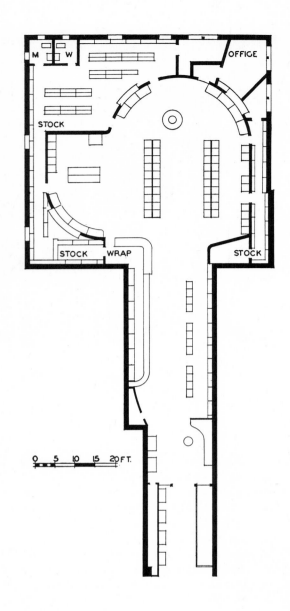

THE PROBLEM was to add a new, larger sales salon to an existing narrow store which was also to receive a new front calculated to lure customers inside. The result is a varied and pleasant succession of spaces ending in the salon shown on page 163. See also plan at left.

The entrance features a jet black sandblasted wood plank wall which serves as background for the small, waist-high display cases (below) which are complemented in turn by the mass display in the large window opposite.

Three types of lighting add variety to the scheme, the curving pattern of downlights in the salon being particularly effective.

THE PRINCESS SLIPPER SHOP

Jackson, Miss.

Joseph W. Molitor

A STORE FRONT DESIGNED TO REDUCE VEILING GLARE

Siegel's, Grand Rapids, Mich.

Wilfred P. McLaughlin, Architect; Kenneth C. Welch, A.I.A., Associate Architect

Sᴜᴄᴄᴇssғᴜʟ present-day store window design must normally eliminate, or reduce as far as possible, distracting glare caused by the reflection of surrounding outdoor objects. Siegel's, a luxury-apparel-gift store, makes an honest and straightforward effort to do just that. The accompanying sketches and photographs show the architects' studies and their final solution — a geometrical arrangement of glass in reference to normal and important viewpoints so that only surfaces of lower brightness are reflected.

There are many ways that the successful elimination of veiling glare can be accomplished. Mr. Welch presents various solutions to these problems in his article "Reflection Factors in Store Windows," in Aʀᴄʜɪᴛᴇᴄᴛᴜʀᴀʟ Rᴇᴄᴏʀᴅ, July 1946.

Briefly, it has been established that the point of "apparent veiling glare" is reached when the ratio of brightness * of the principal surfaces being reflected to that of the surfaces being viewed through the glass is unity (one to one). In this case the veiling glare is just barely apparent and may be called a quite satisfactory condition. Increases, however, in this ratio naturally result in

---

* Brightness, measured in foot-lamberts, equals the amount of light, measured in foot candles multiplied by the reflection factor, which is the percentage of total light reflected.

Photograph at left, taken about noon in late summer, illustrates effectiveness of slanting display window drawn in section at right. Note how 90° vertical glass in end of shallow display and in door reflect sunlighted objects and buildings, completely obliterating display. Objectionable veiling glare in slanting window (moving bus, white line in street) is above normal display height. Section at right indicates reflection angles and brightness of both show window display and environmental objects. Architects made every effort to highly illuminate background to attract attention and emphasize form by silhouetting merchandise.

an increasingly unsatisfactory condition. When the ratio of reflected to viewed brightness reaches two, a condition results which can be called the threshold of destructive veiling glare. When a ratio of five is reached, an unfortunate glare condition arises which completely destroys the primary function of the display. This condition may easily result when a clear sky, or some light sidewalk, street or building surface, with medium reflection factors, is reflected in a store window.

Obviously, as has been done with Siegel's, a necessary preliminary to store window design is a thorough analysis of the given site with relation to its solar orientation and the brightness of surrounding elements such as sidewalks, streets and buildings which, if reflected, can destroy display values. The type of store, its time of daily and seasonal peak load and the class of customers to which it appeals must also be considered. Pertinent to the final solution for Siegel's, which does its luxury business from 11 o'clock in the morning on and does less business in summer than in Spring and Fall with peak load in December, was that shadows cast on streets were greatest during peak sales periods.

Kenneth C. Welch Photos

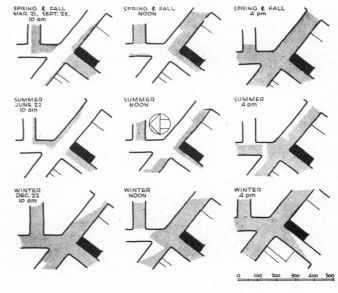

Right: Architects made plan drawings of site and surrounding structures with shadows cast for spring and fall, winter and summer as part of thorough evaluation of brightness environment. Photograph bottom right, made during August about noon, confirms environmental studies, illustrates how angle of reflection (shown on section below) falls within street shadow. Canopy protects display window glass and sidewalk from sky and cloud glare, window shoppers from rain, snow and morning sunshine

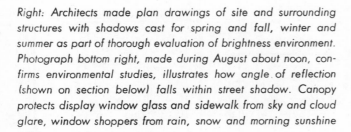

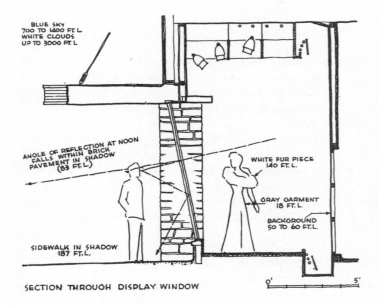

SECTION THROUGH DISPLAY WINDOW

EXPANDING STORE CREATES DESIGN PROBLEM

Carol Antell, New York City

Seymour R. Joseph of Joseph and Vladeck, Architect

THIS NEW YORK SPECIALTY SHOP has approximately tripled its area since it first opened. Its method of expansion was unusual: first, half the ground floor of a former garage was acquired; then a year later a two-story building two doors away was added; and finally the two were linked together. The three-phase development provided an interesting design problem for the architect, and his solution brought him the First Award in the commercial classification at the 1950 convention of the New York State Association of Architects.

First part of the project was the Accessory Shop (extreme right on plan and sketch, photos on pages 90-91). Designed for the display and sale of costume jewelry, blouses and handbags, it is straightforwardly open, with cases lining both long walls. Much of the display area is in the deep entrance arcade, which has a large circular showcase as well as counter-height cantilevered cases on both walls.

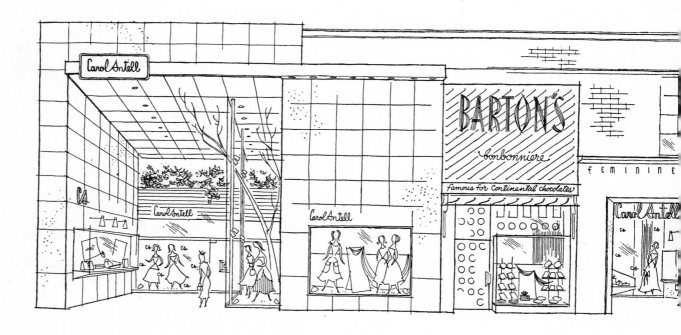

Next came the Sportswear Shop (left on plan and sketch, photos on pages 92-93), which occupies all of the two-story building. Everything about this shop was designed to suggest the outdoors — the two-story arcade, the flagstone floor, the tree growing out of the show window, and the pool in the rear of the store. (Offices and stockrooms are on the second floor.)

The last and most difficult phase of the expansion came when half the space between the two shops was acquired, along with a continuous area to the rear which permitted a connecting passage. This new space was utilized for facilities such as stock and alteration rooms, fitting rooms, and wrapping desk. The connecting passage itself also permitted the use of surfacing materials as a visual link between the two quite different shops.

Exterior walls of both shops are precast terrazzo block; interior walls are plaster, wood panels, and Tennessee ledgestone. Ceilings are plaster and redwood, floors are carpeted in sales areas. The architects designed all showcases and fixtures, and selected everything that went into the entire shop — even to the ashtrays.

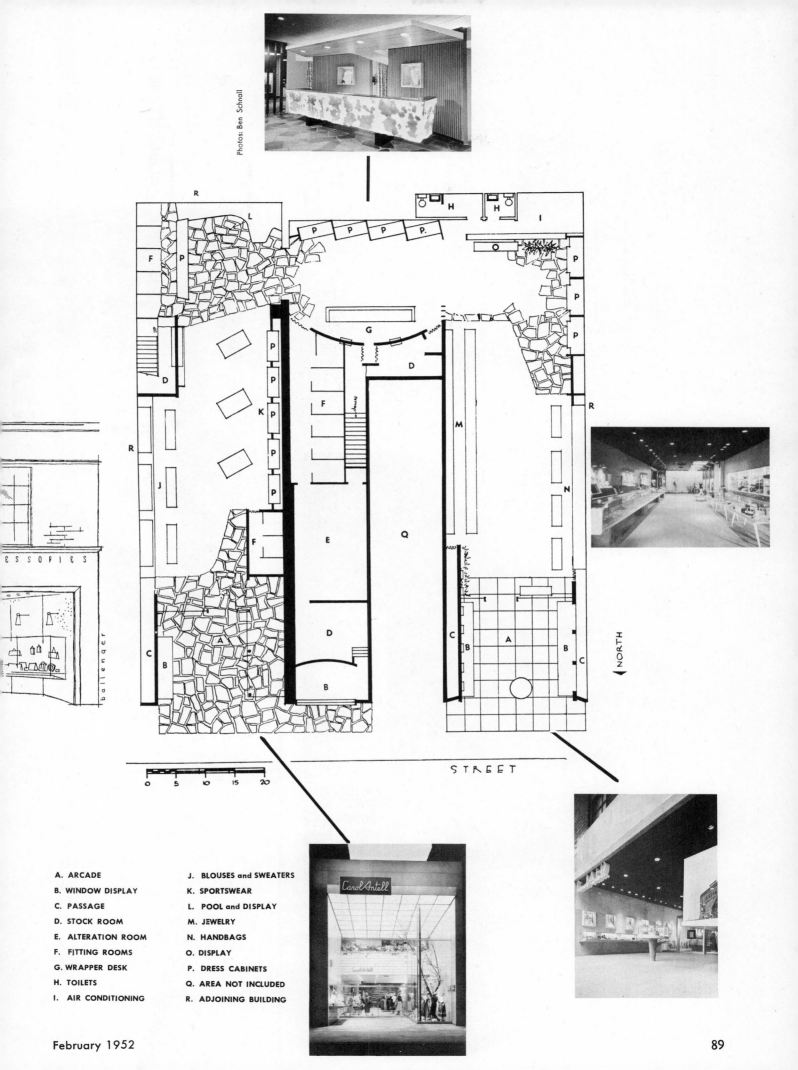

STREET

NORTH

0   5   10   15   20

A. ARCADE

B. WINDOW DISPLAY

C. PASSAGE

D. STOCK ROOM

E. ALTERATION ROOM

F. FITTING ROOMS

G. WRAPPER DESK

H. TOILETS

I. AIR CONDITIONING

J. BLOUSES and SWEATERS

K. SPORTSWEAR

L. POOL and DISPLAY

M. JEWELRY

N. HANDBAGS

O. DISPLAY

P. DRESS CABINETS

Q. AREA NOT INCLUDED

R. ADJOINING BUILDING

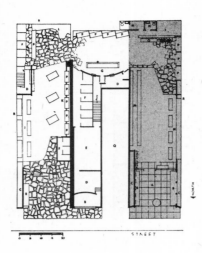

The Accessory Shop, first part of the store to be completed, has plaster walls and ceiling, concrete floor. Mirrors on jewelry counter are mounted on universal joints, can be swung down behind counter. Rear wall is illuminated glass panel with mirror spots

CAROL ANTELL—ACCESSORY SHOP

Three circular show cases (details and photo opposite) were designed by the architect especially for this shop; a fourth, mounted on a tapered pedestal, is used in the arcade (left)

Photos: Ben Schnall

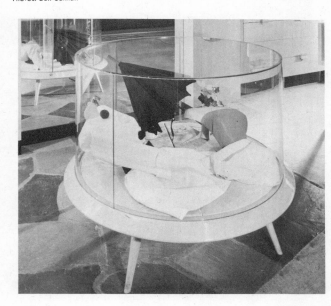

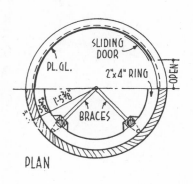

PLAN

SLIDING
DOOR

PL. GL.
2"x 4" RING

1-5⅜"

OPEN

BRACES

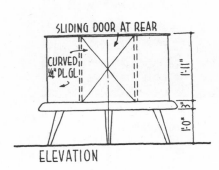

SLIDING DOOR AT REAR

CURVED
¼" PL. GL.

1'-11"

3"

1'-0"

ELEVATION

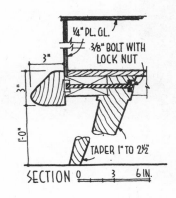

¼" PL. GL.

⅜" BOLT WITH
LOCK NUT

3"

3"

1'-0"

TAPER 1" TO 2½"

SECTION 0   3   6 IN.

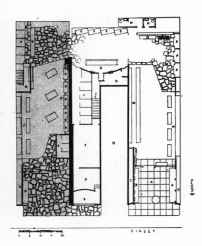

Second part of property acquired was a two-story building which offered more freedom in design of exterior. Since this is a sportswear shop, an outdoor atmosphere was desired. Hence the flagstone floor in arcade, the tree growing out of show window. Side walls here are wood panel, rear wall is Tennessee ledgestone

CAROL ANTELL—SPORTSWEAR SHOP

Photos: Ben Schnall

Ledgestone wall is clearly visible from street, adding to outdoor emphasis of planting box on second-floor balcony. A few fitting rooms and stairs to second-floor offices are behind stockroom desk (top, opposite page)

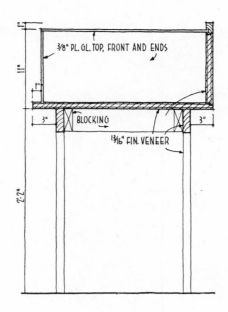

3/8" PL. GL. TOP, FRONT AND ENDS

1'1"

1"

3" BLOCKING 3"

2'2" 13/16" FIN. VENEER

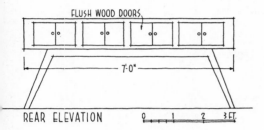

FLUSH WOOD DOORS

7'-0"

REAR ELEVATION   0   1   2   3 FT.

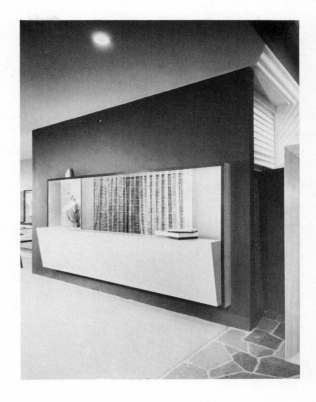

The architect designed all showcases and fixtures, cantilevering most of the wall cases. Flagstone floor of arcade is carried into interior and repeated in rear of shop which connects with Accessory Shop (next page)

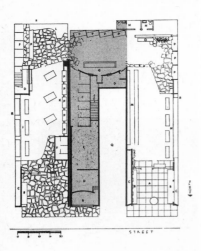

CAROL ANTELL—CONNECTING PASSAGE

The two shops were tied together visually by repetition of certain materials, particularly in passage between them, where common facilities such as wrapping desk are located. Wrapping desk is covered in cowhide, which is repeated on bench at rear of Accessory Shop (page 91) Note small pool in extreme corner of Sportswear Shop (right)

Photos: Ben Schnall

CURRENT TRENDS IN STORE DESIGN

by Morris Ketchum, Jr., A.I.A.

of Ketchum, Gina and Sharp, Architects

AFTER a period of slow progress during the war and depression years, retailing has now embarked on a full-fledged building program. In every branch of trade — from specialty shop to department store — new building projects are on the drafting board, under construction, or newly completed. The encouraging feature of this new era in store design is the high quality of its planning. Thanks to the stern training of the war and depression years, merchants and their architects are now building stores that are realistic answers to the demands of contemporary merchandising.

Today, store designers and their clients are fully exploring — and solving — the inter-related problems of the indoor and outdoor shopping street — sales and services, advertising and display, pedestrian and auto traffic, walkways and parking spaces. In addition, a real start has been made in solving the problems of our blighted city shopping districts and in creating new, *decentralized shopping centers* built for the drive-in trade. This is perhaps the most significant current trend.

In our cities, the problem of the small retail shop is being restated in fresh, new terms. Designers have long since realized that the basic fundamental of store planning is *flexibility* — in the planning of the indoor sales space (and its behind-the-scenes operational activities). The current trend is to organize each sales floor for flexible free-flow of horizontal traffic and for centralized vertical traffic, which provides an efficient merchandise transportation system for incoming stock and outgoing deliveries. Flexibility is furthered by equipping the sales space with stock fixtures that have many interchangeable parts and uses. Another major trend is the integration of sales space and sidewalk displays by a visually open store front that — for the sake of flexible change of pace — may become a closed front whenever closed window backgrounds are installed.

For maximum flexibility and adaptability, the current trend is to reduce to the absolute minimum those structural elements that form the fixed shell of the store building — columns, floor slabs, shaftways, etc. The remainder of the structure — the finish floor surfaces, ceilings and partitions — that enclose sales, services and displays — are being designed as dry-built, knock-down units capable of multiple use and providing flexible access to the space and equipment they enclose.

Two other important trends are worthy of special note — the increasingly effective lighting of both store and merchandise, and the year-'round air conditioning that provides customer comfort and retailer profit. The examples of non-glare, high-level lighting (without distressing brightness contrasts) show both imagination and engineering skill in using light as an integral design factor and a sales adjunct.

All this progress is evident in the current crop of new shops and stores presented in this issue. Perhaps the most striking examples are those

branch department stores that, by their highway location and drive-in facilities, have made it possible for their parent stores in the heart of the city to expand horizontally. Stores always follow the crowd — there is no mousetrap philosophy to retailing — and these stores are following their decentralized customers out to the suburbs.

The chief problem facing any department store is to give its customers the same cheerful personal service, the same leisurely selection, the same glamorous sales atmosphere offered by its smaller rivals. The problem is not an easy one, but careful attention to the individual design of each sales department and to the overall relationship of all departments on the floor has successfully created, in these new branch stores, the atmosphere of an indoor collection of specialty shops instead of the warehouse atmosphere of a bargain basement devoted to a volume trade. Behind the scenes, an equally careful study of operational requirements has given the sales force more freedom from routine, more time for personal salesmanship.

Next, the smaller shops and stores located in the heart of the city prove that it is still possible to give a fresh answer to the problem of high rentals, restricted space, and a store front almost limited to two dimensions. Within their own slice of shopping environment, each of them has solved the eternal problems of maximum interior efficiency, exterior advertising and display, individuality and character. Their store buildings are necessarily part of the weird, accidental pattern common to all our city shopping districts. There is little or no chance for light, air, or spatial development around each store. Instead, their designers must do their best to appeal to the passing crowd by taking every advantage in width, height, and depth of the limited display frontage at their disposal. Then, when they are all through, a curbed parked truck may hide all their efforts, destroy all the sparkle and glamour of their sidewalk show.

The list is long and varied, but most of the stores shown appeal to women shoppers. This appeal is visually expressed in the architecture of store fronts and sales floors — in the refined elegance and conservative luxury of the perfume salon, the carefully controlled mass displays and open hospitality of the popular-priced dress shop, in the open showcase character of the mid-block shoe stores. All these shops, regardless of their individual showmanship, have one trait in common — the promise that shopping will be a leisurely, pleasant experience spiced with personal attention from the sales force and an entertaining background and atmosphere.

The men's clothing store strikes a different note on the same theme. Its store front emphasized privacy tempered by hospitality, its sales floor is organized like the lounge of a men's club. It successfully combines "sample selling" with variety sales of furnishings and clothing. Materials, textures, colors and lighting all combine to make its men customers feel at home.

The camera, flower, jewelry and liquor shops — all selling more to the general public than to a particular age or sex — rely on emphasizing the specialized appeal of their respective merchandise. Each one has solved its own problems of site, location and layout; all represent a better than average answer to the small store problem.

These selected examples of current progress in the field of store design give an encouraging picture of its future. Today's demand for increased shopping facilities is being met by a larger group of trained designers than have ever before devoted themselves to this branch of architecture. Despite the fact that some find it hard to free themselves from the use of imitative design cliches and from the temptation to "busy" their solutions with unnecessary and distracting detail, all have realistically attacked the problems involved. Their shops and stores are cleanly organized, well equipped and well related to the shopping environment around them. With such a high average today, tomorrow's stores should mark the full maturity of design for merchandising.

Morris Ketchum, Jr., has collaborated further by analyzing and commenting upon most of the selected stores shown in the following pages

LORD AND TAYLOR'S WESTCHESTER STORE

Starrett & Van Vleck, Architects

Raymond Loewy Associates, Designers

George A. Fuller & Co., Builders

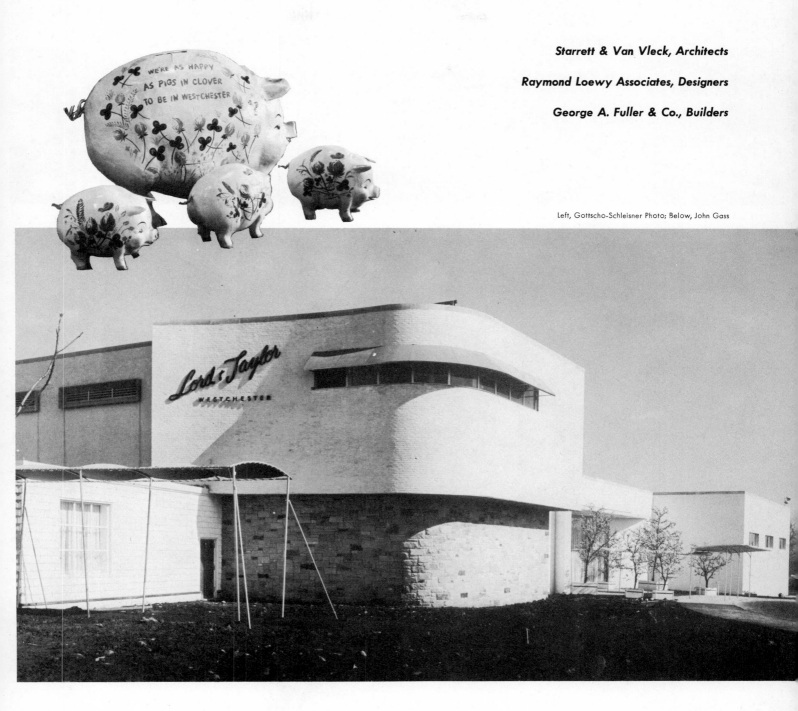

Left, Gottscho-Schleisner Photo; Below, John Gass

AMERICA's newest and most inviting store opened its doors, and blocked traffic for miles, the last week in February. It is a model of smart advanced design and incorporates many of the newest most effective contributions to the art and science of retail merchandising. An atmosphere of cheerful well-being is created by the open, airy, light, colorful, free-flowing interior design. The planning gives each merchandising department its own appropriate and individual milieu and decor while maintaining a consistent unity of spirit and a gay harmony of pastel color. Settings are successfully designed to augment the display of the merchandise itself, not to compete with it. And the store is as efficient as it is attractive, for the facilities for delivery, storage, distribution, marking, wrapping, etc., have been arranged to save steps, time, space and handling. — *M. K., Jr.*

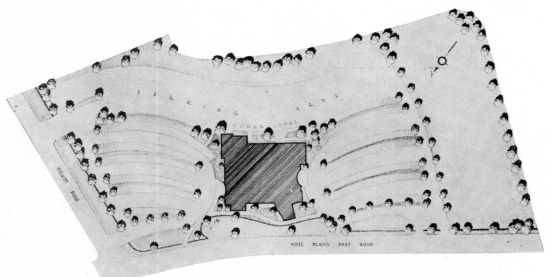

Plan of the site showing parking. W. Lee Moore, Landscape Architect

An easily-accessible, centrally-located suburban site was chosen for the store at White Plains and Wilmot Roads in an uncongested neighborhood. Parking for 1000 cars is provided and buses go past the door. The plan shows the well-arranged parking facilities and eventual attractive landscaping. Above, the south-west corner and canopied entrance. Left, looking south along the White Plains Road or west side of the store

There are two selling floors, and, due to the contours of the site, both are accessible by car. The lower level on the east side (or rear) of the store is shown above; the receiving department and truck loading area are at the north-east corner. Below, the south entrance, executive offices, employee's lounge and lunch room open on the wide roof deck of the second story

Gottscho- Schleisner Photos

1

Gottscho-Schleisner Photo

Above, the dignified setting for "better fashions" opens to the east of the high, glazed, south entrance. Below, looking toward the south entrance from the "Young New Yorker" department; stair to lower floor in foreground. Opposite, the semi-circular area of the "Young New Yorker" section. The planning of stock rooms, fitting rooms and other off-stage services is worthy of careful study. Accessibility, efficiency, and flexibility are apparent. Numerals refer to camera locations on the plan

2

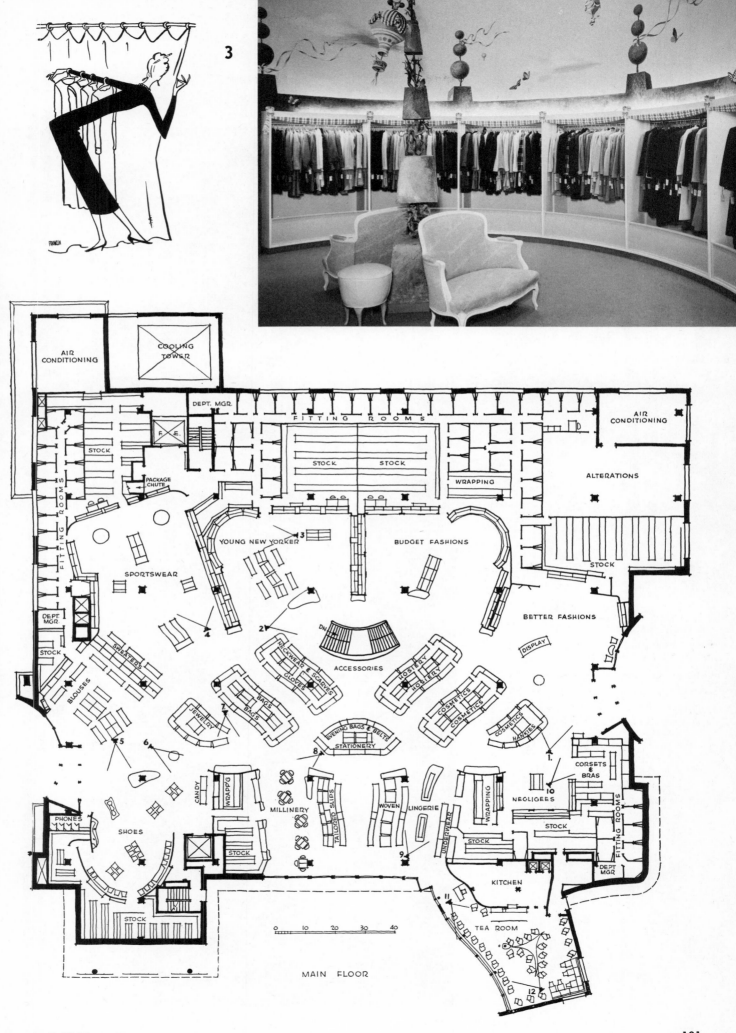

3

AIR CONDITIONING

COOLING TOWER

DEPT. MGR.

F I T T I N G   R O O M S

FITTING ROOMS

STOCK

F. E.

PACKAGE CHUTE

STOCK   STOCK

WRAPPING

AIR CONDITIONING

ALTERATIONS

STOCK

YOUNG NEW YORKER   **3**

BUDGET FASHIONS

SPORTSWEAR

BETTER FASHIONS

4

DEPT. MGR.

2

DN.

ACCESSORIES

DISPLAY

STOCK

NECKWEAR & SCARVES

GLOVES

HOSIERY   HOSIERY

SWEATERS

COSMETICS

BLOUSES

JEWELRY   BAGS

7   BAGS

COSMETICS

COSMETICS

HANKIES

5   **6**

EVENING BAGS & BELTS

STATIONERY

8

1.

CORSETS & BRAS

10

NEGLIGEES

PHONES

SHOES

CANDY

WRAPP'G

MILLINERY

TAILORED SLIPS

WOVEN   LINGERIE

UNDERWEAR

WRAPPING

STOCK

FITTING ROOMS

STOCK

STOCK

9

STOCK

DEPT. MGR.

KITCHEN

11

0   10   20   30   40

TEA ROOM

STOCK

12

MAIN FLOOR

5

The interior decorating of the store was executed by Edgar Tallman, store decorator, and head of Lord and Taylor's interior display department. A series of spontaneous amusing sketches, by Warren Franklin of the interior display department, adorns the curtains of the fitting rooms

6

4

Page opposite, the gay Parisian street-scene mural enlivens the shoe department, and the painted drape enframement of the candy display graces the turn of a wall. Above, white clapboards, yellow shingles and rustic furniture give an outdoor air to the display of sports clothes. Below, dream-fantasy architecture painted on the curved wall as a background for night-robed mannequins, one of James Patton's attractive murals

7

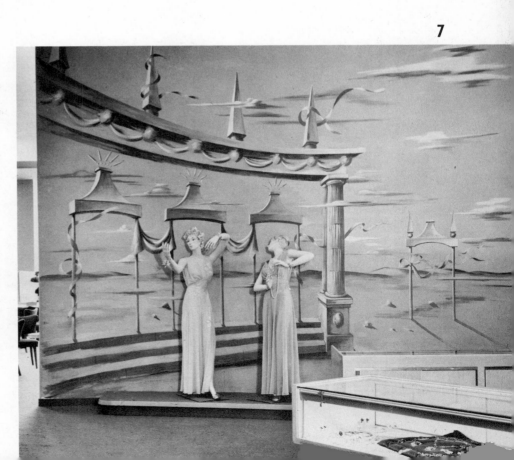

8

9

The quality of the interior design, which is orderly but free, and uses color and light to such good effect, produces a psychological lift in the spirits of all who enter the store. There is a light, sure touch in the decorations which are subtly amusing and never obtrusive, and shoppers are put in a pleasant frame of mind by the bright colorfulness evident throughout. Both natural and artificial light are used to create this bright, cheerful atmosphere, and light is always concentrated on the merchandise. Racks of garments are brilliantly lighted so that the colors of the dresses and hats are part of the decorative effect. The floor is softly carpeted in a pleasing taupe which is neutral and blends with the light pastel shades of the walls and fixtures. *M. K., Jr.*

Opposite page, above, hats in the brilliant niches are held by amusing cupids. Extensive stock is accessible to the clerks through the draped door. Opposite, below, lingerie shelf-doors are painted to simulate beveled construction and are interlaced with painted ribbons and flowers. Yellow stool tops add a bright note of color. Below, the corset department at the left of the south entrance features its laced-corset chairs in brown and pink with appropriately upholstered fronts

10

TEA ROOM PLAN

11

The popular tearoom, flooded with daylight and sunshine, is made colorful by upholstery of blue, chartreuse and rasp-berry, with a floor of striped terrazzo. Supplementary light, when necessary, is supplied by both indirect coves and diffusing downlights. Opposite, the plan of the lower floor shows its main entrance to the east. Directly opposite the foot of the stairs the toy counter is painted as bright children's blocks, and above are clever cut-outs of favorite animals

12

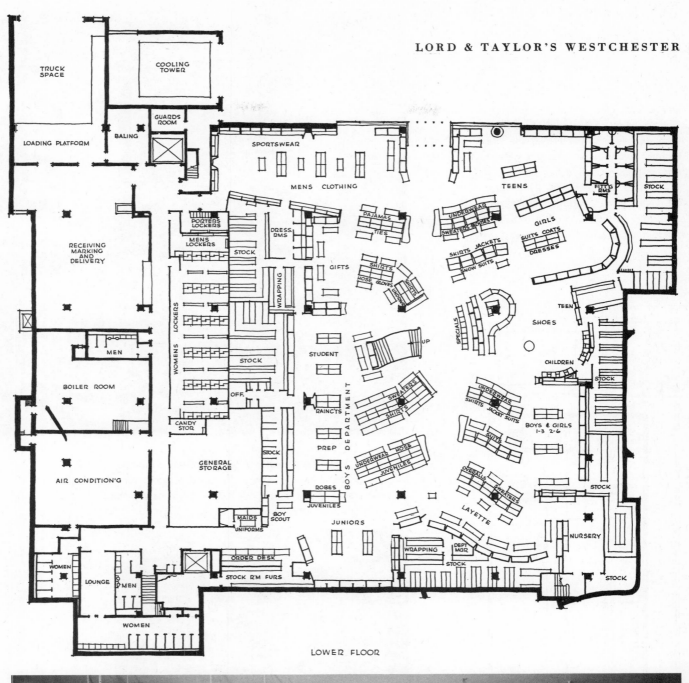

TRUCK SPACE

COOLING TOWER

GUARDS ROOM

LOADING PLATFORM

BALING

RECEIVING MARKING AND DELIVERY

MEN

BOILER ROOM

AIR CONDITION'G

WOMEN

LOUNGE

MEN

WOMEN

PORTERS LOCKERS

MENS LOCKERS

WOMENS LOCKERS

CANDY STOR

GENERAL STORAGE

MAIDS

UNIFORMS

OFF.

STOCK

STOCK

STOCK

STOCK

WRAPPING

DRESS RMS

GIFTS

STUDENT

RAINC'TS

PREP

ROBES

JUVENILES

BOY SCOUT

ORDER DESK

STOCK R'M FURS

BOY'S DEPARTMENT

JUNIORS

SPORTSWEAR

MENS CLOTHING

PAJAMAS

TIES

SHIRTS

HOSE GLOVES

SHIRTS

UNDRWR

UP

SWEATERS

SHIRTS

UNDERWEAR

JUVENILES

HOSE

WRAPPING

DEPT MGR

STOCK

SPECIALS

TEENS

UNDERWEAR

SWEATERS BLOUSES

SKIRTS JACKETS

SNOW SUITS

GIRLS

SUITS COATS

DRESSES

TEEN

SHOES

CHILDREN

UNDERWEAR

SHIRTS JACKET SUITS

SUITS

OVERALLS SWEATERS

LAYETTE

BOYS & GIRLS 1-3 2-6

STOCK

STOCK

NURSERY

STOCK

STOCK

FIT'G RMS

STOCK

LOWER FLOOR

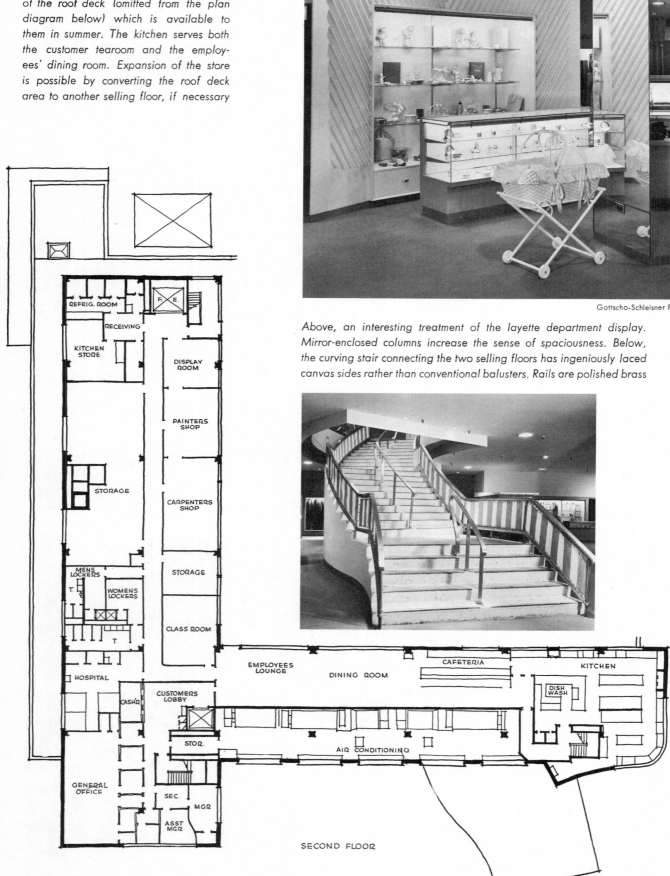

The employees' lounge, dining room and cafeteria open on to the wide expanse of the roof deck (omitted from the plan diagram below) which is available to them in summer. The kitchen serves both the customer tearoom and the employees' dining room. Expansion of the store is possible by converting the roof deck area to another selling floor, if necessary

Gottscho-Schleisner Photos

Above, an interesting treatment of the layette department display. Mirror-enclosed columns increase the sense of spaciousness. Below, the curving stair connecting the two selling floors has ingeniously laced canvas sides rather than conventional balusters. Rails are polished brass

REFRIG. ROOM
F. E.
RECEIVING
KITCHEN STORE
DISPLAY ROOM
PAINTERS SHOP
STORAGE
CARPENTERS SHOP
MENS LOCKERS
WOMENS LOCKERS
STORAGE
CLASS ROOM
HOSPITAL
CUSTOMERS LOBBY
CASH'R
STOR.
EMPLOYEES LOUNGE
DINING ROOM
CAFETERIA
KITCHEN
DISH WASH
AIR CONDITIONING
GENERAL OFFICE
SEC.
MGR
ASST MGR

SECOND FLOOR

Julius Shulman Photo

BULLOCK'S PALM SPRINGS STORE, CALIFORNIA

Walter Wurdeman and Welton Becket, A.I.A., Architects

THIS drive-in department store, located in a winter resort, is another — and very different — example of the trend toward large-scale decentralized shopping units. Although the principal entrance for the automobile trade is on a rear parking court, design interest has been centered, perhaps by force of habit, on the sidewalk approach. Spaciousness, sunlight and hospitality are more important here than the token displays of seasonal merchandise. — M. K., Jr.

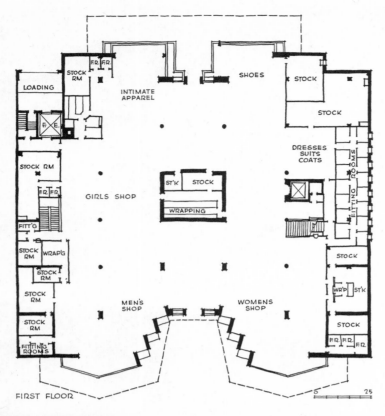

FIRST FLOOR

Julius Shulman Photos

The store's bold planes and masses, bathed in sunlight, stand out against a rugged setting of mountains and palm trees. Symmetrically placed wings enclose an attractive entrance patio. The vertical louvers of the second floor are designed for sun protection to lessen the air conditioning load. Materials and colors, outdoors and in, are in harmony with the store's shopping environment. — *M. K., Jr.*

Wide roof projections shield the large show window bays from the hot sun, and colorful curtains provide supplementary light control

April 1948

The heating and air conditioning system is of the ''reverse cycle'' type having three freon compressors equipped with water-cooled condensers; three vertical shell and tube water chillers; circulating pumps, deep well pump, etc. Ten air conditioning units are placed above the suspended ceilings of the store and are used for both cooling and heating

Expert planning of sales departments gives each an individual character and distinction in spite of the absence of dividing partitions. Cabinet work and lighting are smoothly handled; sales backgrounds are gay and colorful. Note that the merchandising program — apparel and home furnishings — is keyed to holiday demands. Low counters and open planning permit use of a skeleton crew in slack season. There is no attempt to include all the shopping goods shown in a complete department store. — M. K., Jr.

The use of small movable display and storage cases instead of long counters permits flexibility and easy reorganization of sales areas. Display cases are spotlighted from the ceiling rather than lighted from within. Wood is mostly natural and bleached narra

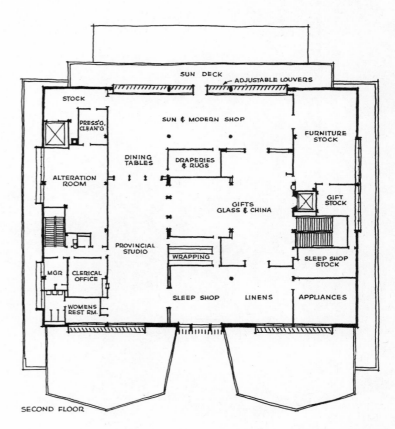

SECOND FLOOR

Four floors of remodeled seven-story building directly serve the public. Exterior is faced with American travertine, with recessed planting boxes (section below) to add floral notes according to the season

Ben Schnall Photos

FOUR FLOORS C

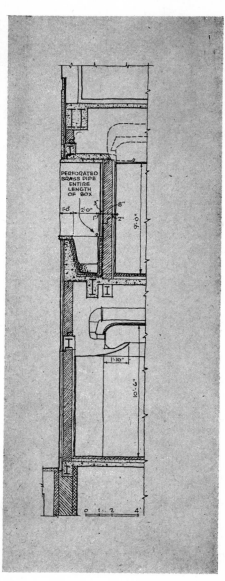

PERFORATED
BRASS PIPE
ENTIRE
LENGTH
OF BOX

SALON LENTHERIC,

New York City

Harrison & Abramovitz, Architects

Ruby Ross Wood, Interior Decorator

Lighting by Feder

HIGH-FASHION SELLING

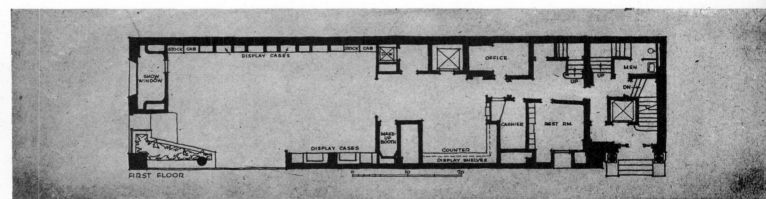

FIRST FLOOR

THE formal, trade-mark approach to "exclusive" retailing here reappears in a new and refreshing solution. High-fashion goods and services are given appropriate sales backgrounds, lighting and equipment, though the goods and services cover an abnormally wide range. In this salon, featuring the Lenthéric perfume, there is a considerable range of women's trinkets and clothing items, and even a men's shop. From a rather severely conservative exterior, relieved by open show windows, the note changes, following the client's wish that the salon have "a mood of quiet tranquillity, with the odor of fresh flowers and sweet-scented greens," and that it be flooded with sunshine. So the lighting tends toward a warm rosy glow designed to make the customer feel beautiful, though in the Men's Corner there is a shift to something a bit more rugged. First floor merchandise, besides the perfume, includes accessories and jewelry; the second floor is devoted to women's clothes, the third and fourth to the hair dressing salon. The shop is entirely air conditioned. (See section opposite.)

April 1948

Right: Men's corner has luminous egg-crate ceiling with high-intensity slimline lamps to simulate outdoor brilliance. Walls are honey-colored leather, carpeting is beige color.
Below: First floor interior in the Salon Lenthéric, with smoky antiqued mirrors and recessed display niches, each with vertical slimline tubes recessed behind a new plastic

Ben Schnall Photos.

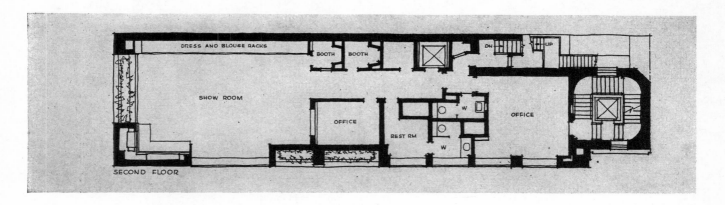

SECOND FLOOR

View of second floor, devoted to at-home clothes, negligees, dinner dresses and so on. Carpet is pink-beige, banquette is gray-beige velvet and gray-beige curtains are of silk gauze. Recessed wall display cases are trimmed with bleached wood picture frames. In the lighting, pastel shades of cold cathode tubing were employed to achieve a delicate, light pink color cast designed to be flattering to customers

Gottscho-Schleisner Photos

CAMERA STORE FOR PHOTO ART COMPANY

Trenton, New Jersey

J. A. Fernandez, A.I.A., Architect

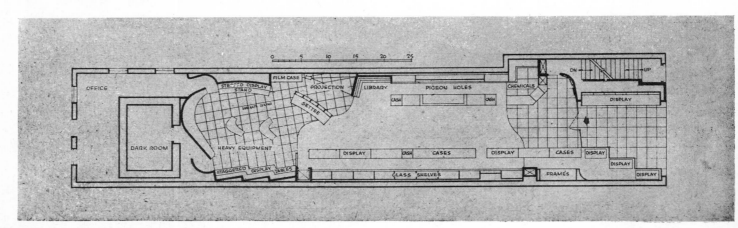

Store front is of gray structural glass, vestibule ceiling is plaster painted pale yellow. Interior woodwork is pickled oak, wall above cases is sea green and ceiling is pearl gray. Main flooring is black asphalt with deep green strips inset

THE high standards set for small shops during the last decade are exemplified in this mid-block camera store. Well-organized signs, displays, sales and services create an over-all effect suited to the specialized character of the goods on sale. Only the slight confusion of multiple lighting and display systems might seem to detract from the essential unity of the design as a whole. The diagonal film racks form an interesting pattern and the larger paraphernalia is well displayed at the rear of the store. — M. K., Jr.

Jan Hankowski Photos

SELBY
SHOE STORE

West Palm Beach, Florida

Igor B. Polevitzky, A.I.A.

Architect

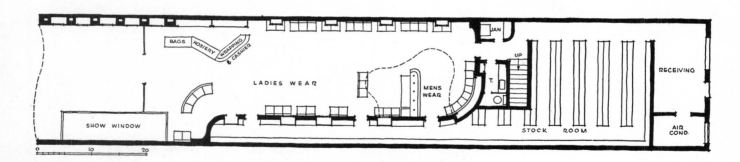

BAGS HOSIERY WRAPPING CASHIER

LADIES WEAR

MENS WEAR

SHOW WINDOW

JAN

UP

T.

STOCK ROOM

RECEIVING

AIR COND.

0   10   20

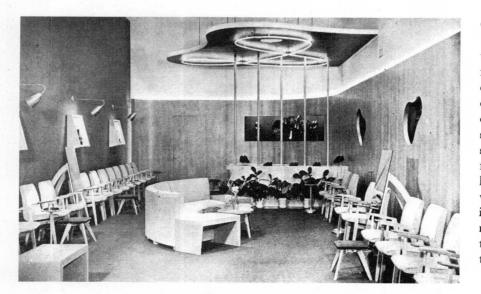

THIS shop and the one on the page opposite prove that the possibilities of the open front store are far from exhausted. This Florida store combines refinement of design and construction with eye-catching colors and textures (the rug is a deep sea green). The edge-lighted lucite sign along the west wall continues from the exterior through the glass line into the store. The glass line is well back from the street minimizing disturbing reflections, an arrangement augmented by high intensity interior lighting which serves the same purpose.

— M. K., Jr.

BOSTONIAN
SHOE STORE

Chicago, Illinois

Morris Lapidus, A.I.A.

Architect

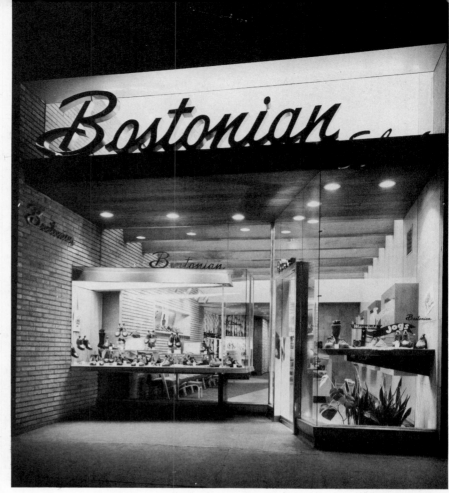

Hedrich–Blessing Photos

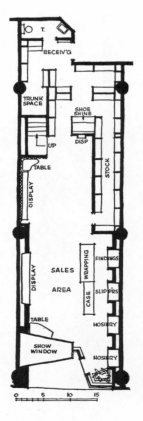

THIS Chicago shop achieves drama and distinction by a bold treatment of signs, backgrounds and displays. The silhouetted sign provides unmistakable identification by day or night and at considerable distances. Maximum show window display is attained in a very narrow frontage by the ingenious placing of the main entrance door at a splayed angle. Heavy beamed ceiling and exposed brickwork contribute to the masculine atmosphere of the store. The beams conceal indirect uplighting sources for the white ceiling above. Supplementary downlighting on the displays increases their sales effectiveness. — M. K., Jr.

Julius Shulman Photos

TO SELL TAILORING FIRST, THEN MERCHANDISE

Carver's, Custom Tailors, Los Angeles, California

Burke & Kober, Designers

THE reserved, almost barren, exterior of this exclusive men's shop is in striking contrast to the luxurious treatment of the interior sales room. A few sales fixtures designed like pieces of residential equipment, massive display racks, soft carpets, colorful greenery, brick and woodwork, a hospitable blaze in the fireplace — all help to create the friendly atmosphere of a lounge. Fabric samples are discreetly displayed in a rear alcove. Behind the scenes, fitting and stock rooms, offices and workrooms, are efficiently arranged. The club-like atmosphere of this establishment is typical of a popular trend in marketing men's wear. — *M. K., Jr.*

Since the impulse merchandise is a secondary consideration to the custom tailoring, the facade was designed to permit a view into the main sales room, rather than to display men's furnishings. Exterior is Red Ark Fossil marble (more brown than red), with stucco above marked off and finished as cast stone. Trim around tempered glass doors is Macassar ebony. As the client did not want any "commercial effect," the main sales area was designed as a lounge, with the furnishings housed in equipment designed like furniture. The studio rooms have north light, but the large skylight in the woolens room is artificial, with a combination of fluorescent and incandescent lighting. Second floor is a large tailoring shop, with skylights

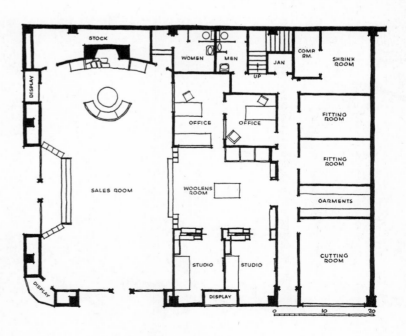

The shop itself is its own show window. The slightly recessed and angled front invites the passer-by to pause and enjoy without being buffetted by other pedestrians

Ben Schnall Photos

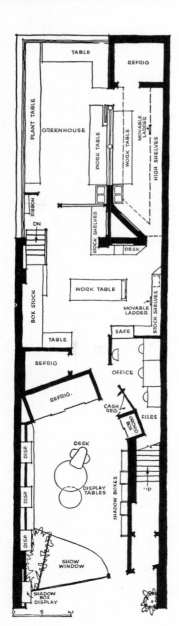

SMART FLORIST'S SHOP, NEW YORK

Marvin J. Neivert, Architect

A STRIKING example — in materials, textures, colors and lighting — of the trend towards greater richness for open-faced shops. That perpetual problem — the separate building entrance — is successfully solved. Sales and service elements, including necessarily large work spaces and the rear greenhouse, are well coordinated. Signs and store front are better handled than the somewhat complicated pattern of overhead lighting or the self-important "free-form" wall cases. — M. K., Jr.

LINDEL'S JEWELRY STORE, TOLEDO

Bellman, Gillett and Richards, Architects

AN open, sheltered front, the mass display of sparkling merchandise, high intensity lighting, thorough air-conditioning, and a straightforward plan for sales and services all add up to an effective bid for a volume trade. Inside, there is very little attempt to give separate identity to each sales department or to soften the somewhat mechanical floor pattern, except the slightly angled setting of side cases toward the entering customer. — *M. K., Jr.*

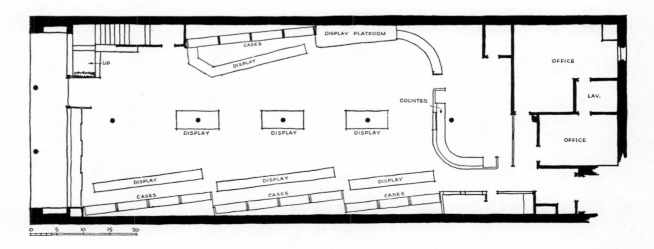

Floyd Ray Photos

COMPANION SHOPS WITHOUT CONFUSION, LONG BEACH, CAL.

Kenneth S. Wing, Architect

Plans show both the Irene Burke store and the Guild House, I. Miller store (illustrated on the following page). Each shop is distinctive and different, but compatible with its neighbor

THE two stores together can outfit milady from top to toe, but they are entirely separate entities under separate proprietors. From a design point of view they are complementary rather than clashing. A good example of luxury retailing, the intimate Irene Burke shop offers its patrons feminine merchandise and personal salesmanship against appropriate and colorful backgrounds. Sales floor flexibility is, perhaps justifiably, sacrificed to a formal arrangement of sales departments, each in its own setting. Equally intimate but more spacious interior effects can be achieved if boundary partitions are kept lower than ceiling level, but higher than eye level. Outside, the rich texture of brick and marble make an excellent foil for the interesting tri-part pattern of show windows — only the oversized canopy and sign letters seem to be unnecessarily large and heavy for so feminine a shop. — M. K., Jr.

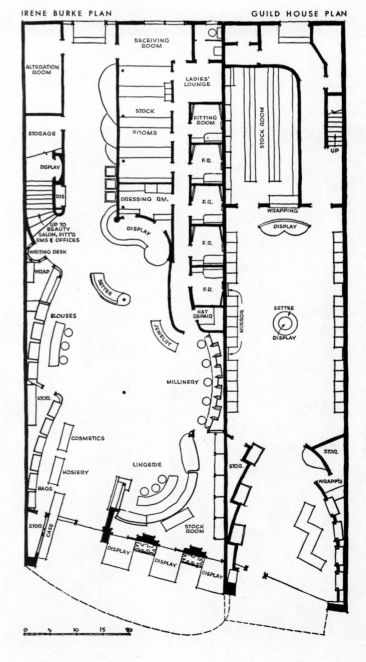

IRENE BURKE PLAN   GUILD HOUSE PLAN

The raised letters of the signs cast shadows contrasting with their surfaces and increasing legibility by both day and night

Floyd Ray Photos

THIS shop is a good companion to its next door neighbor (shown on preceding pages). Indoors, shoe sales and reserve — the demand department — are properly placed at the rear, impulse accessories at the front, for maximum customer traffic and display value. This arrangement also gives the sales floor an air of privacy in spite of the visually open front. The high point of both interior and store front is the well-organized and detailed accessories section. Indoors and out, lighting, textures, colors, all contribute to the shop's intimate appeal. Recessed store front and canopy are more consistent in scale as compared to its next door neighbor. — *M. K., Jr.*

Above and below: to make most effective use of the very small area of Robert Liner's shop, the 35-ft ceiling had to be lowered. This was done—meeting city codes and keeping expenses to a minimum—by stretching clothesline cable from wall to wall and hanging sheets of corrugated aluminum. Corrugated aluminum was used also on curved rear wall

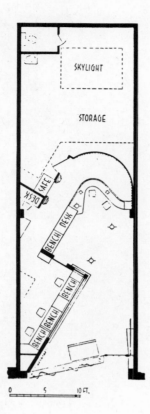

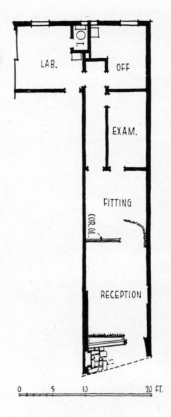

ROBERT LINER
WATCHMAKER SHOP

Beverly Hills, Calif.

Mark & Joyce Sink, Designers

Attention in this long and narrow watch-maker shop is focused on the four watch-makers, their instruments and their activities. The sales area, normally close to the entrance, is behind and to one side of the work-room, but clearly visible from the door. Small though the total floor space is (16 by 50 ft), a sizable area in the rear was salvaged for storage.

H. J. BURKHARDT
OPTOMETRIST SHOP

New York City

S. J. Glaberson, Architect

With a frontage of only 9 ft, this small shop was designed to be as open and attractive as possible, and have the character of a professional office. Space was so limited that all rooms had to be dimensioned carefully for the equipment each was to contain. The examination room, for instance, had to be long enough for use of the chart, but in such tight quarters had to be kept to the minimum.

AN OPTOMETRIST'S SHOP WITH OPEN VISION

Wilmington, California   *Louis Shoall Miller, Architect*

AN optometrist's office naturally should be well lighted throughout in keeping with "Better light, better sight." By day or by night the shop designed by architect Miller is attractively lighted. The recessed entrance is open and inviting as well as distinctive in its simplicity and in the nice choice and use of materials. Brick is particularly well used, both for floor and walls within the building line. The glass show case is adequate and effective for showing the small objects to be displayed, and it serves also as a screen for people sitting in the waiting room, as they can still look out without being the objects of attention. A small planting strip adds color and a more friendly, intimate character to the entrance. The low display case will be noticed by those who may be using the upper floors though its sharp protruding corners must be avoided.

Floyd Ray Photos

The cove-lighted reception room is inviting and comfortable. Utterly simple in design, it gains its character from the warmth of the V-jointed Philippine mahogany paneling, simple wall covering and soft, quiet carpeting

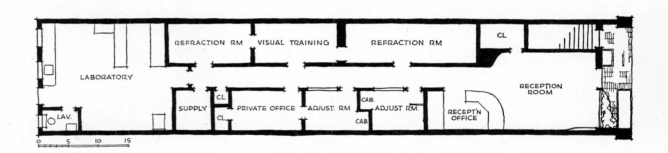

The lot is long and narrow and for the optometrist's purposes the plan is divided into small functional rooms on **either** side of the corridor which leads ultimately to the laboratory. The reception office is well placed for directness of control

Richard Garrison Photos

VISUALIZING THE TROPICS

Beeston, Stott, Patterson, Designers

**Office of the Panama National Tourist Commission
New York City**

IN a limited space, Panama is effectively dramatized and made alluring, an exotic tropical atmosphere is created, and provision is made for pre-vision of the delights of the country through moving pictures. And there is still room for the necessary offices and the mail department. The decorative mural map with its bas-relief accents separates the reception and display space from the unadorned projection room, and the waving palms complete the tropical setting.

Plan, section, and view of projection room show the efficient simplicity of the arrangements for inviting prospective travelers to "stay awhile in Panama"

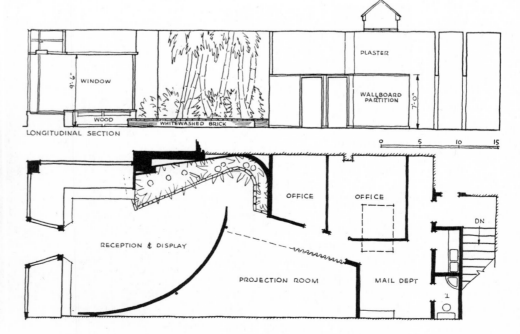

LONGITUDINAL SECTION

RECEPTION & DISPLAY

PROJECTION ROOM

OFFICE

OFFICE

MAIL DEPT

There can be no mistaking which of the two shops is for men and which for women. The Roman brick facade and single show window of the former are sturdily masculine, the arcade and individual show cases of the latter are undeniably feminine

Gruen and Krummeck —

Victor Gruen, Architect

WHERE ONE STORE EQUALS TWO

C. H. Baker Shoe Store, Glendale, Calif.

SINCE men purportedly are shy about passing through ladies' hosiery and bag departments to reach their own bailiwick, this shoe store catering to both men and women has been divided into two entirely separate shops, each specifically designed for its own clientele. Each has its own entrance and its own character. Roman brick forms the exterior of the men's shop, with display limited to a single large show window. The women's store features an arcade with Travertine walls and individual rectangular show cases, and a glass wall at the end of the arcade opens up a view into the interior. Inside, a partition firmly separates the two, and as far as the customer is concerned the departments are independent units. The service facilities, however — stock rooms, wrapping desk, etc. — are so placed that they serve both sections.

Chairs in the men's shop (left) are covered in maroon plastic; walls are light ochre, carpeting is a medium green. Below: another view of the women's salon. Service facilities are used jointly by both sections

A good view of the women's salon (below) is provided passersby by the glass wall at the end of the arcade (right). Walls in this section of the store are dusty rose, chairs are covered in dark green, and carpeting is in a medium green

Julius Shulman Photos

PROTOTYPE FOR A SHOE STORE CHAIN

COWARD SHOE STORE

HACKENSACK, N. J.

Sanders, Malsin and Reiman, Architects

THE ESTABLISHMENT of architectural motifs to be used as a trade mark was the paramount design consideration for this small shop. The owners of the parent store desired a simple, easily recognizable building which would serve as a prototype for a branch chain of children's shoe shops, to be built in several eastern communities. The architects developed a simple facade, dominated by a sign of stained wood and plastic letters, patterned after the label insignia used by the store. Child-appeal was given to the durable, easy-to-keep interior by the introduction of bright colors, and plastic clotheslines to support lighting coves. Special consideration was given to minimizing upkeep, display and operational problems for a limited staff.

Shop windows are divided into sections by cypress siding to simplify window decoration. Window bases are white opaque glass. Fascia beneath sign houses awning. Entire shop interior is visible from street when curtains are opened; it was found, however, that most customers prefer privacy

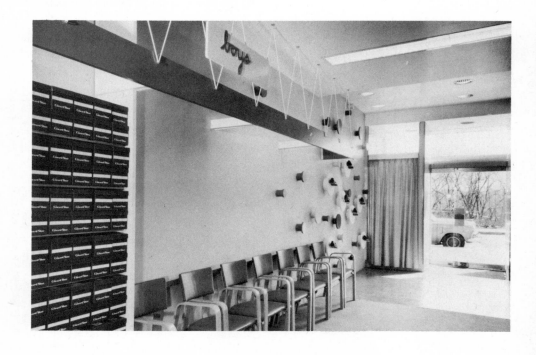

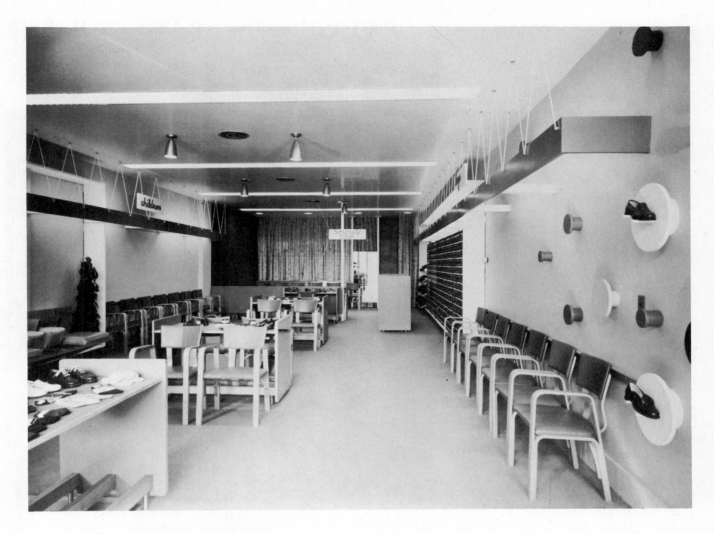

Ben Schnall

Interior walls are light gray, deep brown. Accents are brilliant colors. Shoes and boxes are prominently displayed to simplify selection. The stock room is located behind whimsical curtains at rear of shop. Air conditioning and other equipment is in basement

Joseph W. Molitor

DRUG STORE

Jackson, Mississippi
N. W. Overstreet & Associates, Architects

A CIRCULAR GLASS-ENCLOSED STAIR, angled show windows, and a wire trellis over the parking area give this store and office building in Mississippi a look of light openness very welcome in the South.

The building, designed by Robert K. Overstreet, an associate in his father's firm, is in a suburban business section of Jackson. The main floor is an unbroken sales area; glass walls along the north (parking) side and across the front permit customers to see the whole store as they enter, whether they arrive by car or by foot. The druggist, too, has a clear view of the entire floor from his office — a balcony at the rear, beneath which is tucked a florist's shop opening to the parking area. Storage space is in the basement.

The second floor of the building (plan next page) consists of several suites of doctors' offices, complete with laboratories, X-ray and fluoroscopy rooms. An elevator is provided for the use of patients who do not wish to or cannot use the circular stairs at the front. Those stairs, of course, are not merely an attractive feature of the building, but a sound merchandising feature as well: from them the second-floor visitors get a full view of the store's displays.

The exterior of the building has a flair about it which again indicates the merchandising sense of the architect. Over the parking area is a trellis of aluminum wire and stock steel shapes trimmed to a delicate profile; vines eventually will cover the wires, cutting down show-window reflections and providing a cool greenness. Across the front is a reinforced concrete canopy, roughly triangular, from which protrude decorative aluminum rods.

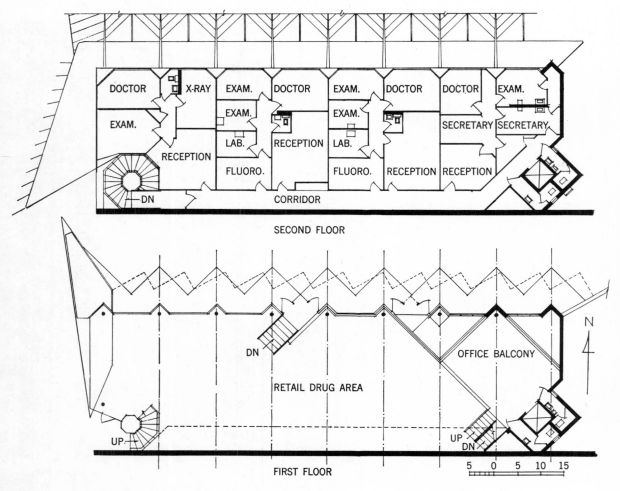

SECOND FLOOR

FIRST FLOOR

DN

UP

RETAIL DRUG AREA

OFFICE BALCONY

DOCTOR · X-RAY · EXAM. · DOCTOR · EXAM. · DOCTOR · DOCTOR · EXAM.

EXAM. · EXAM. · EXAM. · SECRETARY · SECRETARY

LAB. · RECEPTION · LAB.

RECEPTION · FLUORO. · FLUORO. · RECEPTION · RECEPTION

CORRIDOR

5 0 5 10 15

Druggist's office balcony is 5 ft above main floor;
site slopes to rear, permitting florist's shop below
balcony. Heating and air conditioning equipment
is in basement. Building is reinforced concrete,
built-up roof, 4-in. glass wool thermal insulation

Joseph W. Molitor

COUSINS FURNITURE AND APPLIANCE STORE

Johnson County, Kansas   *Kivett & Myers, Architects*

THE SITE of this store is on a highway leading to one of the better residential sections of Kansas City. Half of the building formally was a supermarket which was badly damaged by fire and subsequently remodeled; the other half (left on plan below) is new. The second floor show window was the result of the owner's request for display space which could be seen by approaching motorists from the top of a nearby hill.

Foundations are stone (old portion of the building) and concrete block; exterior walls are red brick.

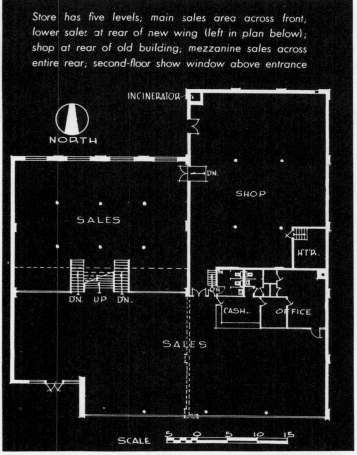

Store has five levels; main sales area across front; lower sales at rear of new wing (left in plan below); shop at rear of old building; mezzanine sales across entire rear; second-floor show window above entrance

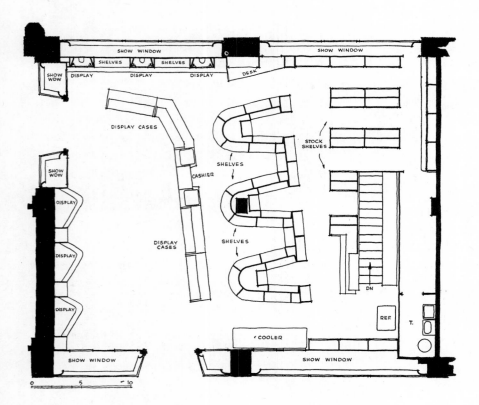

Haskell Photos

LIQUOR MART, NORTH STATION,

BOSTON, MASS.

David J. Abrahams

Architect

THE outstanding feature of this interior modernization is the tremendous stock capacity gained by careful replanning. The design of the clean-cut sales counter is also commendable. It is unfortunate that in the photograph the rectangular lighting pattern of the ceiling seems to compete with the curved lighting of the stock shelving. Materials, colors, customer traffic and behind-the-scenes services are all well handled. **Morris Ketchum, Jr.**

SHOPPING CENTERS

Introduction

The sudden mushrooming of suburban shopping centers is one of the most interesting aspects of the postwar building boom—for here is a new concept and a new building type non-existent only a few years ago which is now abuilding at crossroads all over the land. Where did these come from and why? What happens downtown when one is built in a suburban fringe? Have any sound planning principles been evolved? The answers to these and many other related questions are of interest to architects when they enter upon this extremely active field.

In a recent news story, the Urban Land Institute had this to say, "It is true that the central portions of cities are not growing rapidly. Increases in population are taking place in the suburbs and in the fringes outside corporate city limits. With this new pattern of urban growth, shopping centers are coming into being by reason of the increase in suburban population and the resultant increase in purchasing power located there rather than by reason of any flight of downtown business. The impact of the automobile makes possible a redistribution of expanded commercial and industrial activity over a greater area surrounding the metropolitan core.

"Downtown areas are holding their dominant position . . . by reason of the pulling power built up during the mass transportation era. Whether this magnetism will continue depends on the central business district's ability to safeguard its wide selection of goods and concentrated purchasing power.

"The real resource of downtown is the crowd— the shoppers, the workers, the transients, the public seeking services. The crowd is important to the retailers, the newspapers, the banks, the property owners, to the community as a whole. To hold this asset in an era of individual mobility means that the central business district cannot rely on tradition but must make deliberate improvements.

"The required improvements include freedom from congestion, provision for offstreet parking spaces in ample number, convenient access, better and faster mass transit, attractive modernized build-ings, and attention to the amenities including elimination of garishness, unnecessary noise and impediments to easy circulation. The suburban shopping center incorporates these criteria.

"Established business districts must not only look to their laurels; they must initiate positive action. Otherwise the planned regional shopping center, with its full range and depth of goods for comparison shopping and with its facilities for easy marketing and customer appeal may become a direct competitor of and not a supporting complement to the downtown district."

A prominent architect who is actively engaged in shopping center work has said that the most important single element in successfully designing such projects lies in the architect's state of mind. He explained that the architect must make every effort to approach the work as though he were the *owner* of the project—and design accordingly. This does not imply the giving up of high artistic and professional standards; on the contrary, they must simultaneously be held at the highest level. To express it in another way—the center must *first* be planned for successful financial operation and within this discipline should then provide all the amenities and attractiveness possible.

Comprising information in this vein which should prove both useful and interesting to architects, the main body of our text will present the latest ideas of owners, market analysts, real estate men, and merchandising consultants insofar as these ideas bear directly upon the activities of the architect. Certain portions of the recent study on the subject compiled by the Urban Land Institute, Max S. Wehrly, director, will be quoted. Additional material from our own or other sources will be interspersed in *a different type face* to amplify certain points.

---

* Technical Bulletin No. 20, Shopping Centers; Planning Principles and Tested Policies Based on Experience from the Community Builders' Council. Compiled by J. Ross McKeever and published by the Urban Land Institute, Washington, D. C. $6.00.

L shape two-level shopping wraps around a free-standing Macy
"puller" in Architect Victor Gruen's Bay-Fair, San Francisco

Harry H. Baskerville

A Place to Begin

The present day shopping center began as an experiment to go with suburban living.
It grew out of the early Sears and Wards branches built on a lot with a place for
parking customers' cars. It evolved from a single unit into a series of stores under
one management. Then, later, the series took on clear characteristics as try-outs became successful practices. Early developments were the ventures in Baltimore at
Roland Park, in Kansas City by J. C. Nichols, in Dallas by Hugh Prather, in Houston by Hugh Potter. The pioneers of the Twenties and Thirties created the pattern
for the merchandising phenomenon that is the shopping center of today.

The development of shopping centers has progressed . . . to the extent that such
construction . . . can be called a building type. Even so, there is not much long-
term practice to set hard and fast rules. At best, we have rules of thumb. But developers . . . have tested theories about shopping center planning based on their
own experiences. An account of experience is a good place to begin.

The planning and operation of a shopping center include more than high hopes or
hunches. The development has moved from a single operation to one involving research, planning and promotion by a team of specialists.

first — economic analysis: Ultimate success will depend upon the care taken to
evaluate the market. Market analysis is the substitute for the golden hunches of the
real estate genius. Hugh Potter says, "When the shopper was at the mercy of mass
transit lines '100 per cent locations' were a safe substitute for market analysis. But
when widespread auto ownership liberated the customer . . . it became evident
. . . that the shopper could be pulled almost anywhere by a strong merchandising
attraction and by what the downtown district so signally lacked — a place to park
the car." The market analysis determines the kind and size of project, and is a job
for an expert in that field.

second — site selection: Decision on the site is the next step, and the decision
relates to all the factors of suitability. These will be discussed in detail later.

Too often the architect is not consulted early enough in the selection of the site when his advice to the owner might be invaluable. Such considerations as shape, orientation, access, slopes, drainage, soil conditions, etc. should be his direct concern from the beginning.

third — preliminary site planning: The next operation includes preparation of preliminary plans for the building and site layout, and requires the services of the architect. The project begins to take form in its eventual adaptation to the physical characteristics of the site and the trade area. Site engineering studies and tests are made to learn the sub-surface conditions. During the planning phase the time is ripe for preliminary negotiations with prospective tenants. After there has been agreement on the land usage of the site, the traffic planning and the merchandising setup, the project is ready to move towards its next stage.

fourth — detailed architectural plans: "Do we want air conditioning; are our costs in line?" At this stage, the project starts shaping toward reality. Final plans must clear with municipal authorities; the architectural, structural, and mechanical drawings assume final form; parking and traffic handling arrangements become fixed; a prospectus is prepared for lease negotiations with tenants. After leases with major tenants are signed, the project is ready to move toward ground breaking and actual construction.

Robert C. Cleveland

What Makes a Shopping Center

In general these are the ingredients for a good shopping center:

A site layout that will provide a store group with minimum walking distances, both from parking areas and within the store group itself

A store group that can be merchandised to provide the greatest interplay between stores

An arrangement that eliminates all poor store locations and difficult parking stations

Separation of foot traffic and automobile traffic and elimination of all service facilities from the public consciousness

A management that is efficient and capable of obtaining cooperation from individual tenants for the benefit of the whole center

A unified architectural building group that looks like a shopping center and not an assemblage of miscellaneous stores.

Omitted from the above listing are the inflections, the interpretations, the innovations that must be made in order to apply these ingredients to your site and . . . local conditions.

Emporium Department Store, Stonestown Center, San Francisco, Welton Becket & Associates, Architects and Engineers

Site Selection

In site selection, the same principles will hold, but in varying degrees, whether the center is to be a small neighborhood development or a regional giant. The points to evaluate are:

location is of primary importance. Hugh Prather, owner-developer of Dallas, says, "The most important point in determining location is to be sure that your site is located near a well populated residential area or one that is growing so rapidly that it gives promise of soon being able to support the size of shopping center you contemplate."

Charles E. Joern of LaGrange Park, Ill., gives these five points in determining location: "Purchasing power to be tapped, stability.of income in the trade area, location and size of competition, future growth, and accessibility."

Another point is added by Walter S. Schmidt of Cincinnati: "The side of the street . . . can spell profit or loss. If the center is in an outlying area, retail stores should be on the right side of the outbound street to catch going-home traffic."

access is a very important consideration. Mr. Schmidt says, "A location at the intersection of two heavily traveled highways is not the best. If entrances and exits are too near a major intersection, the interference with through traffic can create a congestion problem. Traffic planning must make it easy to turn right into the center. It is better if the location is accessible to major highways rather than on them, though the ability to see the center from the highway is of great benefit for its advertising value."

As for regional centers, Mr. Schmidt adds, "To achieve the maximum accessibility the site should be at, near, or readily convenient to at least two main highways. If the location is adjacent to a high speed expressway, the turn-in facilities are important." A cloverleaf intersection is not best for convenience of access.

Driving time distance plays a leading role in the accessibility of a site. According to studies made by the United States Bureau of Public Roads in cooperation with state highway departments,* most shoppers are reluctant to travel more than 25 minutes by private automobile or more than six miles or 20 minutes by bus. The time element often plays a more important part than mere nearness, especially for the medium sized development. For more careful study of this factor, it is extremely revealing to plot driving times as contours on a map. Such an approach points up the fallacies of the old concentric circle method.

size should be at least sufficient to provide the minimum acreage set up by the preliminary estimates from the market analysis. In estimating area needs, Mr. Seward H. Mott uses these guides as rules of thumb: "For an acre of ground, 10,000 sq ft can be allowed for gross store area. A car parking space takes at least 300 sq ft (including a proportion for travel lanes). On this basis about 100 cars can be parked **per** acre — this allows a 3 to 1 ratio."

The allowance of space to grow is a safeguard for the future, particularly with centers in mushrooming suburbs. Too often, a successful center is built without reserving extra land for future growth — not only for an increase in customer parking but also for additional sales area.

Another note: the site should be all in one piece. Mr. Potter adds for emphasis "Do not divide the shopping area by any cross traffic streets." Note, though, that a *minor* road through a site does not always interfere if carefully handled.

Another factor to consider is the **shape** *of the site, for it can often exert undue influence upon the resulting layout of buildings. Beware of the odd shaped area that can be purchased cheaper, for it may make good planning difficult to impossible, and it is often wise to pay a little more for logical trade lines and shorter walking distances.*

As for **topography,** *the older idea that the flat, open site is best no longer holds. Two-level parking which permits two-level entrance to department stores is today a popular arrangement; some developers even create such a multi-level scheme when they*

* *New York Herald Tribune, March 10, 1953.*

Driving time map reveals fallacy of old concentric-circle distance map in studying site accessibility. The Center, Omaha; see right page

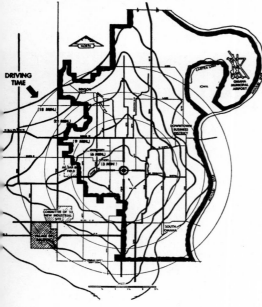

have a level plot. *Under certain conditions, a sloping site can also make construction of delivery truck tunnels easier and cheaper.*

sub-surface soil conditions *should be investigated at the earliest opportunity, for if unfavorable, they may make foundation work unduly expensive. Caution is advisable when such hazards as hydrostatic pressure, rock blasting, deep excavation, or others must be dealt with.*

utilities should ideally be near or in place. The problems of obtaining water, sewers, storm drainage, and power should be looked into before property acquisition proceeds too far.

If utilities are not in place, the cost of bringing them to the site must be added to the cost of the land.

Customer comfort in Nebraska's rugged climate provided by all weather air conditioned shopping space reached from two level parking. The Center, Omaha, Nebr.; Kenneth C. Welch and J. & G. Daverman, Architects, John A. Wiebe Co., Developer

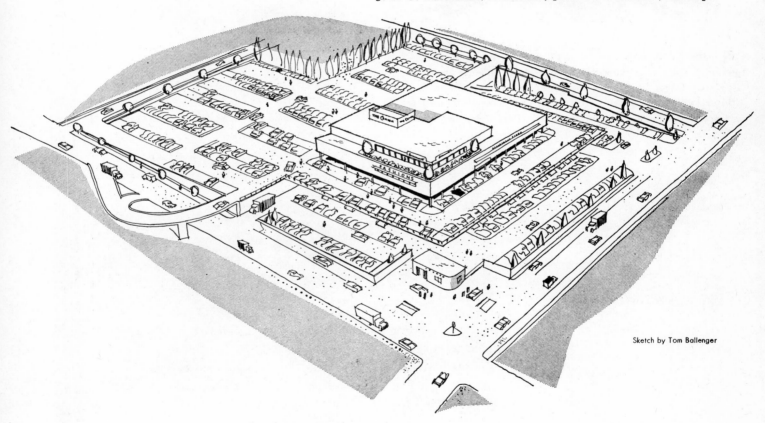

Sketch by Tom Ballenger

zoning for strip business locations along major traffic streets is the usual rule today unless the community has recently revised its zoning ordinance and map. Since such existing locations are unsuitable for the modern shopping center due to insufficient depth and cross cutting streets, new zoning or re-zoning, brought about by petition, will usually be necessary.

Sometimes there may be local opposition to re-zoning a tract of land for shopping center development, particularly if the center is to be close to a built-up single-family residential section. In such a local atmosphere, the developer must sell his ideas to the authorities and to the community. He must judge the local temper

A "cluster" plan with central mall and careful store grouping, above, features Architect Welton Becket's scheme for Hillsdale, San Mateo, Calif., as opposed to the ample garden and patio areas which impart an informal character to Pereira & Luckman's design, below, for Lancaster-Palmdale, California

Spanning a bisecting street with a two-story unit on stilts gains building area with smaller land coverage in The Hub, Hicksville, L.I., Morris Lapidus, Architect

before he goes too far. Where the center is to be located close to existing residences, buffer planting strips are essential to prevent adverse effect upon residential values.

In overcoming local opposition it is sometimes advisable to offer certain concessions to the authorities and the citizens. Perhaps a portion of the site can be set aside as a public park, playground, or for some other community use; sometimes it is wise to have local civic leaders serve on a committee to approve the building and landscaping designs for the new center.

There is a distinct trend in cities to incorporate in their zoning a "shopping center district" — the district defined as "developed as a unit under single ownership." This new use is in line with similar provisions for a "planned community district." Both these "districts" are an attempt to allow for large scale development geared to an overall plan. The objective is commendable for it seeks a way alternative to the conventional provisions of zoning geared to the single lot, and which only indifferently helped to promote large scale development. The waiver of single lot regulations for the above is the way shopping centers should be zoned.

the final choice involves being sure the site is the best possible from every point of view. Weigh the points on this check list:

    1 — Properly located; nearby residential walk-in trade is valuable
    2 — Easily accessible by automobile and bus
    3 — Sufficient size; room for expansion; all in one piece
    4 — The right shape; no grading or sub-surface problems
    5 — Utilities in place or at least nearby
    6 — Favorable zoning
    7 — The right price

Planning the Site

customer circulation

The store grouping starts with thinking about the key tenants and ways to place them so that advantage can be gained from the pull of customers to and through the center. Mr. L. E. Fite, owner-developer of Jefferson Village, San Antonio, points out: "The important thing is to distribute the pull and to lead the customers past the smaller tenants as they are drawn to the pullers."

the number one tenant

In speaking about shopping center problems, Dr. Homer Hoyt, eminent market analyst, makes a useful classification of centers by means of designating their number one tenant. He says, "We may divide them into four types:

Class 1 — The large regional center with large department store (or two)

Class 2 — The center with a junior department store as the largest unit

Class 3 — The center with a variety store as the largest unit

Class 4 — The center with a supermarket as the largest tenant."

For the neighborhood center (Class 4) the Council believes that the best location should be filled by the drugstore with the supermarket placed for convenience to parking. In the suburban or community center, the number one tenant may be either the junior department store (Class 2) or the variety store (Class 3). The Council is thinking of some tenant such as Sears, Ward, or Penney in the department store field. In this kind of center with 20 to 40 stores, it is well to have both the department store and the variety store together with a super food market — each in prominent spots.

In a large regional center, the large department store is the number one tenant — the only variation being whether to have one or two department stores.

In the Community Builders' Council, there has been a lot of discussion about the most valuable businesses in a center. Local conditions naturally cause variations, but the Council finds the most popular types of businesses in existing centers are, in order: drugs; food market; variety stores; bakery; dry cleaner; beauty parlor; women's wear; shoes; gift and bookstores; children's clothing; jewelry; barber; men's wear; candy shop; and shoe repair.

A - SPECIALTY SHOPS
B - MARKET & SHOPS
C - RESTAURANT & PHARMACY
D - JR. DEPT. STORE
E - MEDICAL BLD'G

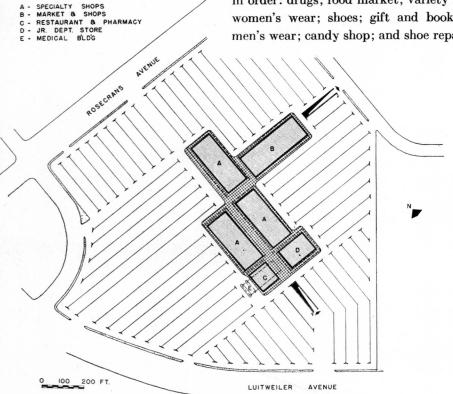

With a supermarket and junior department store at mall extremities, pedestrian traffic is pulled past specialty shops in Welton Becket's scheme for La Mirada, Calif.

Architect Morris Lapidus copes with two bisecting
streets by means of pedestrian overpasses in his design for the Falls Shopping Center, Fallsington, Pa.

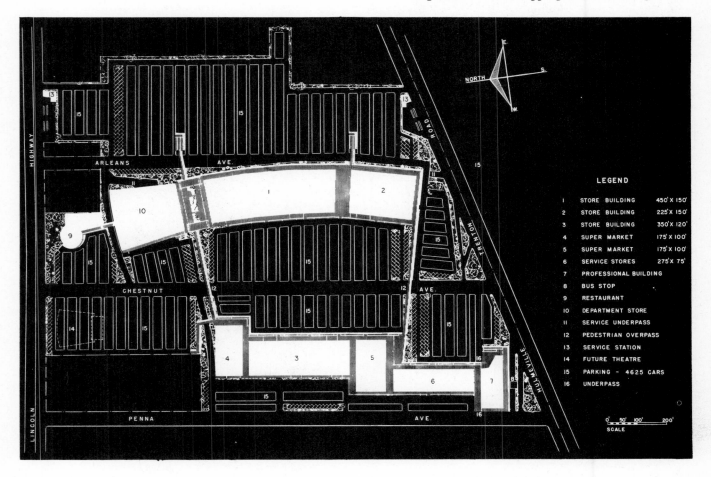

LEGEND

1	STORE BUILDING	450' X 150'
2	STORE BUILDING	225' X 150'
3	STORE BUILDING	350' X 120'
4	SUPER MARKET	175' X 100'
5	SUPER MARKET	175' X 100'
6	SERVICE STORES	275' X 75'
7	PROFESSIONAL BUILDING	
8	BUS STOP	
9	RESTAURANT	
10	DEPARTMENT STORE	
11	SERVICE UNDERPASS	
12	PEDESTRIAN OVERPASS	
13	SERVICE STATION	
14	FUTURE THEATRE	
15	PARKING - 4625 CARS	
16	UNDERPASS	

store grouping — in general

With the number one tenant selected, the next step is the site layout. There are varying arrangements for buildings. They are: the strip, the L, the U, the ring, the mall, and the cluster. Adaptations of these change in order to fit the site. The mall and cluster are more suited for use in large regional centers, while the strip, L, and U are more usual in smaller centers. The ring is rarely circular but rather is descriptive of a group spaced about a central open area.

In designating stores within a grouping, the first consideration is proper selection and arrangement to draw more customers to all the stores.

It is difficult to overestimate the importance of locating the "puller" stores in such a manner that pedestrian traffic is routed past the smaller stores handling impulse items. This makes for the success of the entire center.

Another principle in store grouping lies in taking care that all convenience goods stores are as close as possible to parking. John Taylor remarks, "The grouping of stores in a successful center will be the result of planning store locations so that their relationship one to another will be of the utmost benefit to all."

J. W. York, owner-developer of Cameron Village in Raleigh, emphasizes this idea: "Experience shows that it is the supermarket that helps the department store." Theoretically, it would seem that the department store would be the big frog, but the supermarket is proving to be the department store's best neighbor.

The Council has said repeatedly that stores complementing each other should be placed together. For example, shops catering to women should be close together; service and repair shops may be grouped; groceries, services and 5-and-10's complement each other. In assigning locations to prospective tenants, it should be noted that the Council urges second floor locations for doctors and dentists; or better still, a separate, detached "medical clinic" type of building for them.

An L shaped plan on an L shaped lot which incorporates three department stores and truck tunnel service particularizes the Park Central Center in Phoenix, Ariz., Welton Becket & Associates, Architects

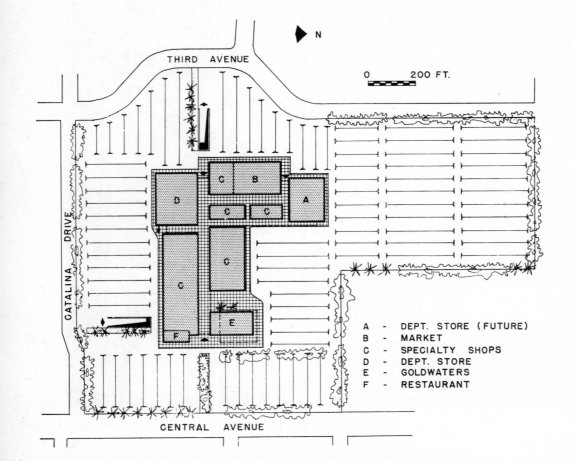

A - DEPT. STORE (FUTURE)
B - MARKET
C - SPECIALTY SHOPS
D - DEPT. STORE
E - GOLDWATERS
F - RESTAURANT

In strictly architectural terms, the site design should be based primarily upon a free flow for four kinds of traffic: shoppers in automobiles; shoppers walking to and from parking; service and freight trucks; and pedestrians within the building group proper. The object, of course, is to eliminate interference between any of these and at the same time provide maximum shopper flow past all the stores so that all the locations become "100 per cent locations."

store grouping in regional centers

In the big center, the architectural plan must place small tenants in the path of pedestrian traffic moving between the larger tenants — department stores, supermarkets and drugstores.

"A regional center must be self-sufficient," Mr. Flaherty emphasizes. This characteristic underlines the importance of proper grouping. This "self-sufficiency" means that in addition to the big pullers, there must be a full range of merchandise available to the shopper — including everything found downtown. This completeness implies competition within the center — which is good for the center and good for the merchants. It keeps merchants on their toes and gives shoppers the comparison they want to be able to make when shopping. James B. Douglas, president of Northgate, says: "Put in two markets, two dress shops, two drugstores."

To say it another way: the center should be like another "downtown," the size of which depends upon estimated volume based on the market analysis. Having competitive stores close together is what makes downtown go — yet this widely accepted fact is sometimes lost sight of in shopping center layouts.

to combine or to separate?

The big problem here comes in locating the stores within the group. For example: is it desirable to group all the food stores or to separate the two supermarkets? This query brings into focus the basic problem of grouping — whether to bring stores

Architects Weinberg & Teare's double bow shaped mall provides a pleasant openness for the O'Neil Sheffield Center, Sheffield Township, Ohio

of one kind into close relationship for convenience and competition or to separate them to spread pedestrian traffic.

When the supermarkets adjoin, the load on the parking space is unduly concentrated; this is one good reason for separation. Placed together, servicing is easier to arrange; besides, comparison shopping is easier for the housewife.

Hugh Prather's experience speaks for grouping: "We put a supermarket and a service grocery together and it works beautifully. Food store grouping is important — they complement each other. In high grade centers women wearing slacks buy groceries in the morning, return for luncheon and go dress shopping in the afternoon."

Mr. Seltzer of Philadelphia also votes for grouping: "In our large center we group fashion shops and have the less expensive type of merchandise in another section. When the department store was asked about having a food store nearby, they replied that they would take *one* high grade food store for a neighbor. The load on parking was the reason for their objection.

The smaller neighborhood center in strip form, with separated service, is illustrated by the Bissell Hills Center, St. Louis County, Mo., as drawn by P. John Hoener & Associates, Architects

Mr. Bohannan favors separation: "At Hillsdale, we dislike putting food stores together even though it may be a service to the public to do so. The parking required is greater than for any other kind of soft line store. We are planning one big supermarket at either end of the mall with a Sears and Penny at either side. Women won't go to two supermarkets on the same day; one-day-a-week food shopping is the trend, and we want to encourage other shopping on the same trip.

Here we find the experts in disagreement about the question of grouping or segregating similar kinds of stores, and no pat answer seems apparent. More experience may tell.

where to place the department store

In a regional center, the department store is the puller. A junior department store should be separated from the large store, as should the second large store, should there be one.

Larry Smith, economic analyst, points out: "The shopping center developer should be sure he gets the maximum benefit from the pedestrian traffic the department store creates. If the smaller stores do not benefit from the foot traffic to and from the large store, the owner has lost the very thing for which he negotiates in signing the department store lease. Be sure that the plan provides maximum benefit to all stores resulting from the pull of the department store."

small service shops

Locating small stores comprising 500 to 1000 sq ft of sales area is important, for these stores pay high rentals, add interest for the shopper, and contribute to the completeness of the center. One suggestion for a frontage location for shops of this type is the pedestrian passageways leading from parking to mall, as at Northgate. In this manner, blank walls are avoided and good spots are provided for the little shops and for impulse buying. Such shops — yarn, dress pattern, costume jewelry — generally receive stock shipments by parcel post and do not need to be directly accessible to truck service.

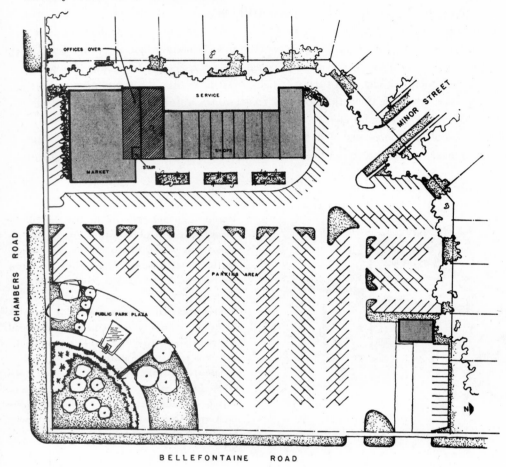

store sizes

Walter Schmidt says: "Store depth should be 100 to 140 ft. A depth of 120 ft is thin for major stores. Many chains ask for 140 ft and self-service drugstores now want 160 ft. Where there are no basements, such stores require nearly as much storage area as sales space. Stores of 125 to 150 ft in depth are needed."

Optimum size for supermarkets seems to run from 18 to 20 thousand sq ft. The Council cautions that supermarkets can become too big; a long trip from the checkout stand to pick up a forgotten item will cause the shopper to go next door or wait until the next trip. The supermarket area is often divided 80 per cent sales space and 20 per cent storage and produce space. Self-service packaged meats reduce the latter figure 65 per cent.

A department store in a center should not occupy more than one third of the total gross building area. In one regional center having a 600,000 sq ft total gross building area, a department store of 200,000 sq ft seems to be about right.

As mentioned previously, a rule of thumb guide for estimating purposes is to figure about 10,000 sq ft of gross building area for each acre of site.

The Necessary Parking

The space for parking is an indispensable element in shopping center design, and in providing it, the two main questions are: how much? and how best to arrange it?

how much parking?

To describe the area needed, a measure has come into being: **the parking ratio.** This ratio is the relationship of the parking area to the building area. The building area may be the gross building area or the net sales area.

For preliminary planning, the ratio of parking area to gross building area is the most practical way of gauging the desirable amount of parking, for it is impossible to determine the net sales area accurately until the building is complete. The attempt to determine a relationship based on complicated formulae of average sales, customers per car, and turnover per car space entails too many assumptions. Ultimately, however, the ratio should be based on the number of car spaces provided for the total sq ft of sales space.

A ratio of car spaces per 1000 sq ft of gross building area (first floor area, basements, mezzanines, and upper floors, but excluding service areas outside the stores,

Renderings and plans of the Waialae Shopping Center, near Honolulu, are shown on these two pages. Victor Gruen, Architect; Rothwell & Lester, Associated Resident Architects; Larry Smith & Co., Economic Consultants.

The open three-part plan will be constructed in nearly equal increments, and the generous site will provide ample parking area and buffer zones.

The structural system features open-web steel joists on a lightweight post and lintel system arranged on a modular pattern. Open-web joists will support tropical flowers and hanging plants

such as boiler rooms, truck tunnels, truck docks, etc.) is an accurate way of arriving at the parking required. A ratio of 2 sq ft of parking to 1 sq ft of gross building area (a 2 to 1 ratio) produces 6.7 cars (say 6) for each 1000 sq ft of building. A ratio of 3 sq ft of parking to 1 sq ft of building area (a 3 to 1 ratio) produces 10 cars per 1000 sq ft of building.

The 2 to 1 ratio is suitable only for a neighborhood center with a high parking turnover and a large percentage of walk-in trade. Elsewhere, the minimum satisfactory ratio is 3 to 1, and more is preferable.

In determining area, at least 300 sq ft must be allowed for each car. This figure includes a percentage assignable to moving lanes. But where there are access drives, pedestrian walks, storage magazine areas and landscaped areas to be incorporated, 400 sq ft per car is the correct allotment for estimating.

At Shoppers' World in Framingham the ratio is 15 cars per 1000 sq ft of store area or a ratio of 4.5 to 1. Such an arrangement is satisfactory even for the December peak.

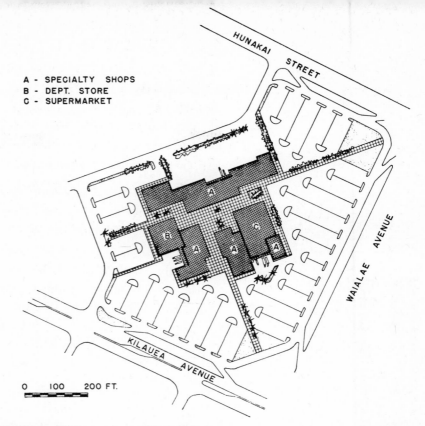

A - SPECIALTY SHOPS
B - DEPT. STORE
C - SUPERMARKET

HUNAKAI STREET

WAIALAE AVENUE

KILAUEA AVENUE

0   100   200 FT.

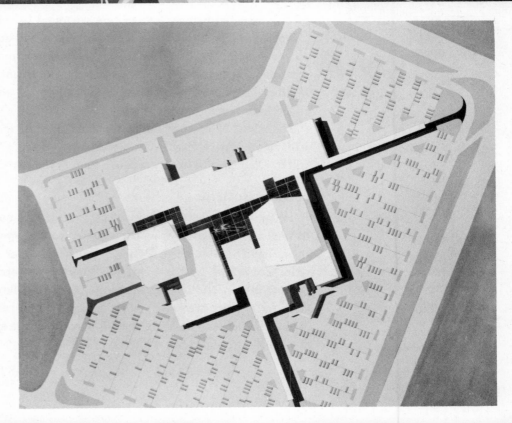

October 1953

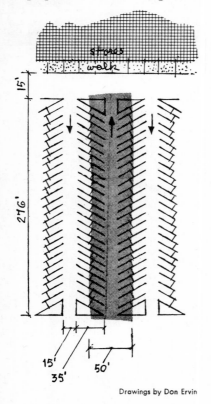

Two preferred parking patterns:
"perpendicular" and "angular"

Drawings by Don Ervin

arranging the space

The act of parking at a shopping center must be simple, trouble-free, and safe. The shopper should be able to find his way around without any previous study of the site. Complicated arrangements confuse the driver and often require directions from attendant (which is expensive for the owner).

Shopping center parking is best a do-it-yourself procedure, because it is cheaper, smoother, entails no waiting, and is best for rapid turnover. The only case in which attendant parking is justified is for the center on expensive land ($3 or more).

As for general arrangement, Walter S. Schmidt says: "Spread the parking to distribute it equally on all sides of the center. People should not have to walk too far to reach the stores from their parking space. Try to limit the depth of parking to 300 or 350 ft each side of the store group."

Ease of circulation and safe movement for pedestrians and vehicles is of paramount importance. In addition, truck service traffic and consumer traffic should be segregated. The best arrangement is one that leads the shopper directly to the stores from his parked car.

Several experts maintain that the main customer traffic should enter and deploy on a peripheral road which acts as a sort of traffic circle for the center, and that traffic near the stores should be discouraged in plan. A completely separated pedestrian walkway next to the stores is a good feature. It is advisable to limit vehicular access to the stores to a few selected key store entrances and a few passenger pickup points. A good scheme is for parking bins to have two-way aisles and open to the peripheral road; this plan keeps all traffic away from the area next the stores except for the few key stations mentioned above. Arcades which pierce through the stores at strategic locations provide a good means of pedestrian access from parking, provided they are spaced close enough to be convenient yet not so close as to create too much unproductive area.

There are two preferred patterns for parking bin arrangements: angle or perpendicular. Perpendicular or 90 deg parking is generally favored because it combines economy of space with ease of circulation. It allows two-way movement, elimination of expensive curbing, better sight lines, and greater safety. When used, a width of 65 ft is required for two tiers of cars separated by a central two-way aisle.

Angle parking allows for easier entering of a stall and for one way traffic and also narrower bays. Where 45 deg parking is used, minimum width of bays can be 50 ft with one-way movement. With two-way movement, 60 ft is required. Angle or herringbone patterns are advisable only for areas where the space is restricted or where local preferences govern.

The width of the parking stall should be 9 ft, measured center to center of a 2-in. painted space-marker line. Mr. J. W. York says, "If you use an 8 ft width, you will lose more space from straddlers than if you mark the area at 9 ft."

pedestrian strips

Raised walkways between rows of parked cars are not needed. Most people prefer to walk toward the shops on the wider car driveways. "Where you have plenty of cheap land," states Hugh Potter, "we should favor putting in a wide pedestrian strip. But where land is tight, we eliminate the strip but usually provide some bumper protection." If such strips are used, they have to be at least 7 ft wide to allow for bumper overhang and the passage of two people abreast. There is general doubt whether walkways are worth the cost and the space involved. Also, they are an obstacle to snow removal.

pavement

Concrete surfacing is expensive, while black-top is satisfactory providing it is well drained. Where there are great expanses of pavement, trees and planted areas should be introduced to eliminate the otherwise barren and unsightly appearance. Best markers for the parking stalls are either painted lines or metal buttons.

employee parking

Short-time and all-day parkers do not mix; and employees are all day parkers. If they are permitted to park indiscriminately, they will be using shoppers' space that

On a heart shaped plot having access from three main roads, Architects Tully & Hobbs have designed the Fairless Hills, Pa., center about an L shaped mall linked by covered walkways

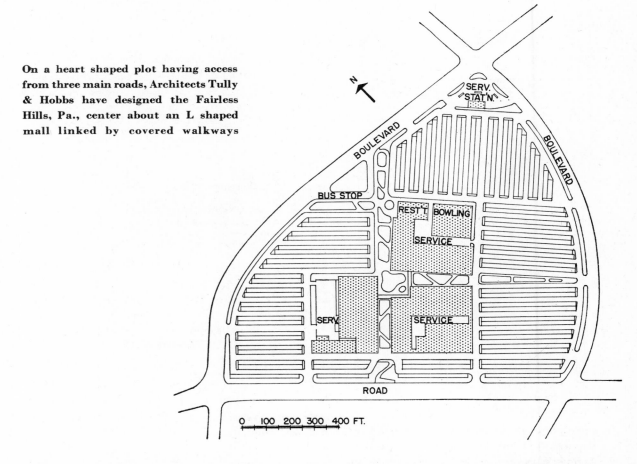

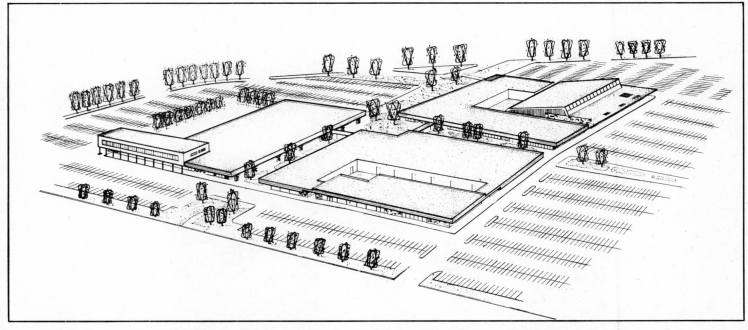

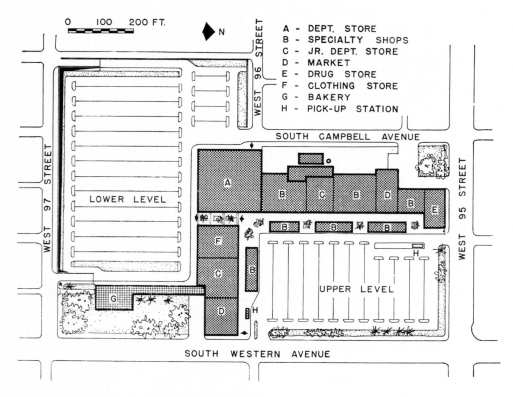

0   100   200 FT.   ◆ N

A - DEPT. STORE
B - SPECIALTY SHOPS
C - JR. DEPT. STORE
D - MARKET
E - DRUG STORE
F - CLOTHING STORE
G - BAKERY
H - PICK-UP STATION

WEST 96 STREET

WEST 97 STREET

WEST 95 STREET

SOUTH CAMPBELL AVENUE

LOWER LEVEL

UPPER LEVEL

SOUTH WESTERN AVENUE

An L scheme served by two level parking which incorporates three main stores characterizes the plan for Evergreen Plaza, Chicago. Howard T. Fisher & Associates, Architects & Engineers; Holabird & Root & Burgee, Architect-Engineer; Arthur Rubloff, Developer

Adjacent to a 100-acre residential development, the Sunrise Shopping Center in Fort Lauderdale, Fla., is located in a rapidly expanding area. Gamble, Pownall & Gilroy, Architects & Engineers

should be turning over four or five times a day. A special area should be assigned to employee parking and violations sternly dealt with.

At J. W. York's Cameron Village we find an indication of the amount of employee parking: "There are 145 cars for 500 employees in a center of 234,000 sq ft gross building area. This means that there are 145 basic cars to contend with, or less than 1 car for each 3 employees."

Services, Amenities

service and the mall

The mall has many advantages for the larger center: it creates a pleasant, landscaped business street free of traffic hazard; it creates many strong locations; there is no "best side of the street"; by double-decking stores along the mall, building area can be doubled without increasing walking distance from parking.

Another point favoring the mall in a regional center is the possibility of the complete separation of truck service and pedestrian shoppers. This is accomplished by building a truck tunnel under the mall, as has been done at Northgate in Seattle, Stonestown in San Francisco, and planned for Northland in Detroit and Hillsdale in San Mateo. But, the truck service tunnel is expensive. "A truck tunnel will cost about $800,000." When the truck service tunnel can be afforded, it offers the ideal solution to the problem of separating customers and deliveries.

Without a service tunnel, the mall scheme requires that service courts be provided. The problem then becomes one of screening the courts from view. Such courts must be large enough to permit truck maneuver within their area, and if not carefully handled, give a "backyard" appearance. The Shoppers' World at Framingham is a regional center with rear courts adjacent to the customer parking areas.

In the smaller center, the difficulty in separating pedestrians and service delivery can hardly ever be justifiably solved by either a mall or tunnel.

landscaping

Planting and seasonal floral displays in appropriate places within the center add to its attractiveness and customer pull. The best advice of the Council is to have some, but since maintenance cost is high, to budget it. Where wide expanses of paved parking area occur, it is advisable to have trees and carefully placed planting. "Barren parking lots are terrific eyesores, and you have to break the expanse."

buffers

When the center is near a residential area, it is necessary to insulate against any adverse effect of commercial use upon the adjacent residential development. A buffer strip at least 20 ft wide and preferably densely planted should be used. "Where such buffers are not possible, the use of walls, solid fences, or narrow but dense foliage should be provided. Failure to install permanent and effective physical separations between business and residential uses will detract greatly from the desirability and value of the latter." For a large regional center, the buffer should be extensive, and can in part be reserved for later expansion.

basements and storage

The answer to the question, "When are basements best?" depends largely on site conditions, such as topography and sub-soil considerations.

Stores require storage space and the basement is good for that purpose. Also, the basement can later be converted to merchandising space should expansion occur. In lieu of basements, balconies are required (necessitating higher ceilings), or the store must be deeper. Another storage device, particularly where stores are shallow, is to provide (on a secondary plot location) a storage building which can be leased to individual tenants according to their needs. Examples are Town and Country in Sacramento and River Oaks in Houston.

Such stores as furniture and variety chains want basement areas for display and merchandising. But basements, like second floor areas, seldom bring an adequate rental, income generally running $\frac{1}{4}$ to $\frac{1}{3}$ of that from the first floor.

In the large regional center basements are a must, and can be scooped out at the same time the truck tunnel is excavated.

second stories

Second floors do not necessarily increase earnings, particularly in neighborhood centers. Extra costs are involved in construction, plumbing, heating, lighting, and maintenance. A two-story center building does not too often pay. Second floor tenants are all-day parkers and their visitors are generally long-time parkers who are not shoppers. It is uneconomical to provide elevators for the second floor.

Doctors and dentists are not the best second floor tenants since the sick patients and healthy shoppers hardly mix well, and a trip to the dentist is seldom combined with a shopping spree.

Should second floor space be provided, the suitable kinds of tenants are those who pull people to the center at regular and frequent intervals; who have visitors who do not park more than an hour or two; and who require no display space downstairs. Dance studios, bridge or language teachers and simiiar occupants are suitable second floor tenants.

package pick-up stations

Handling arriving goods at the center is a problem in itself, usually solved by planned arrangements of service courts, truck tunnels, or rear service roads; but the carrying home of their purchases by the customers is a separate problem. It is far more satisfactory for both seller and buyer if articles can be taken home at the time of purchase. But a bundle-laden female is unlikely to stroll past stores, even to do some window shopping.

An L plan centering on a pedestrian mall in an unusual shape characterizes Architects Weinberg & Teare's scheme for Lyndhurst, Ohio

PROPOSED SHOPPING CENTER
FOR LYNDHURST OHIO

Supermarkets have pioneered with carry-out service. But this is an expensive operation and the real answer must lie in some form of package pick-up station. In operation, the shopper checks her bundles, goes to her car, and then drives to the special station where, in return for a check, an attendant loads her car. The mechanics can vary, but a system can easily be worked out to solve the bundle-toting problem. A sound approach at the neighborhood center level is to have parking as close as possible to shopping.

Variations

service stations in shopping centers are fitting and proper if their location does not interfere with parking lot circulation. They must occupy a prominent place.

We quote Hugh Potter, owner of River Oaks in Houston, which includes two service stations, who says, "You must segregate the filling station area from the customers' parking area. In order to put the filling station in a prominent place, you must have a good-looking structure; it must be kept clean and its traffic must be separated. There is no reason why a properly handled gas station cannot be attractive."

Mr. Bohannon adds: "If you are uncertain about the filling station, you can make a lease of 10 years or so. Lease the ground and take a percentage of sales (about 1¢ per gallon) and other revenues. If the station offers service, it should have an area for car storage."

offices can be better accommodated in a separate office building than in second floors over stores. Such a scheme allows special parking space, separated from the shoppers, which can be easily regulated.

Doctors prefer a one-story clinic type of building or one with elevator facilities. A separate building is best because their professional needs are special and for such they must pay higher rentals. Hugh Potter says: "Whatever you do, do not mix doctors and lawyers in the same building."

An office building brings people to the center, but must have its own parking area and be capable of handling all-day parkers. Provide sufficient site area to handle the special parking and traffic flow to this area.

an automobile row is not good in a shopping center.

banks in shopping centers are great conveniences. They generally pay a fixed rental at a high rate, although one developer reports that he gets $\frac{1}{10}$th of 1 per cent of all deposits as yearly rental. In lieu of a bank, a California development of interest serves as a "currency exchange," which cashes and issues checks. Such a business is good near a large population of factory or defense workers. The exchange takes a small area and pays a high rate — $10 reported by one operator.

bowling alleys are suitable in a secondary location.

church sites should not be selected adjacent to a shopping center just to take advantage of the parking facilities. There is an overlapping in parking use. While churches may well be in the general neighborhood of the shopping center, do not make them a part of it.

theaters, due to television's influence on the economic picture, are hardly a sound tenant in a shopping center.

Above, perspective of the new Bamberger Center in Paramus, Bergen County, N. J., Abbott, Merkt & Co., Architects & Engineers. Below, perspective of River Park Regional Center, Philadelphia, Welton Becket & Associates, Architects & Engineers

Douglas M. Simmonds

168

The trend toward decentralization, long an issue in our major cities, is becoming increasingly important in relation to the imminent expansion of housing to meet defense needs. Greater dispersal of population is also being urged for military reasons. As decentralization continues, steps which will preserve the peace-time economic balance of our cities take on added importance. Business, as well as industry, will have to disperse its facilities to serve the outlying areas. This study brings into focus a number of diverse factors affecting the planning of regional shopping centers which will complement, rather than compete with, existing central business districts. Such centers will serve not only during the emergency period but will also be of permanent value. We cannot afford to build these facilities twice. Fortunately, immediate military and long-range civilian objectives in this instance practically coincide.

REGIONAL SHOPPING CENTERS

By Kenneth C. Welch, A.I.A.

IN THE PAST FEW DECADES many revolutions have taken place that have materially affected our metropolitan areas. There has been a tremendous population increase, accelerated by increased commercial and industrial activities. The impact of the automobile has caused this growth to take place mostly in suburban and even rural areas. The private automobile makes suburban living possible and desirable, even if the wage earner has to commute to the city; the truck permits a compatible decentralization of commerce and industry — which means more jobs for the suburban dweller. Automobiles have also created great problems in the design of highways and parking facilities, which will be discussed in more detail later in this study.

Part of the population of the central cities has also moved into the suburbs. However, the exodus of purchasing power to outlying areas has been relatively greater than the number of families. The 1950 census in the 12 largest cities shows that the population in the central cities has decreased from 60 to 55 per cent of the total metropolitan population in only 10 years. The present median income in the suburbs is $4200, 35 per cent greater than the $3100 of the central area. In the same cities, retail sales in the suburbs increased 217 per cent, but the central city increased only 172 per cent, including the sales of many outlying city store branches and shopping centers.

Retail distribution in the central business districts has also been vitally affected by the fact that many suburbs have a population density too low to support mass transportation. Lack of this increases use of cars, and further aggravates traffic congestion and shortage of parking facilities in the central cities.

These factors have caused the mushrooming of neighborhood shopping centers throughout suburban areas. Parking is less a problem in such locations because adjacent residential streets are used for parking for employees and overflow peaks. Goods are also more convenient to the housewife and shopper. Haphazard planning, however, has led to a bursting-at-the-seams congestion in many of these centers which duplicates, on a smaller scale, a number of the problems of the central districts. The photo at left illustrates such a case, with congested streets, and sidewalks devoid of pedestrian shoppers.

A New Pattern Is Necessary

To help solve these problems, a new pattern of regional retail distribution is needed, based on a planned, constructive decentralization. It would take advantage

SALES POTENTIAL DETERMINES IDEAL SITE

A Typical Study Made for Toledo, Ohio

1. PROPOSED SITE IS CHARTED WITH INFLUENCING FACTORS

of the trends, and create a new type of regional shopping center to fit the suburbs and the automobile. At the same time, it would preserve a healthy central business district. Each center would have a cumulative pull approaching in effect, if not in scope, that of the central district. A series of such centers could be considered branches of the concentrated downtown retail area. Together with the central district, they would serve an entire metropolitan sprawl. The outlying stores would sell to a segment of the region. The central district would operate more efficiently and partially serve the entire area, plus a larger area served by regional transportation. In such a relationship, the regional centers would complement, rather than compete with the downtown stores. Their relation with the community should be carefully analyzed, as shown in the example (above) for a proposed Sylvania-Douglas Center, Toledo, Ohio.

Types of Goods

The types of merchandise and retail services offered in shopping centers differ greatly in their scope, type and power to attract customers from a given time distance. They also vary in relation to purchasing power, impact on the metropolitan area, land and structural use, transportation, and economy.

Convenience goods constitute items bought daily or weekly, such as are found in food stores, drug stores and eating places. It is the kind of merchandise that can be ordered by telephone if delivery service is available. It also includes such services as repair, cleaning, laundry, personal services and health items. The key unit is the combination grocery-meat store. Convenience goods stores are completely dispersed in sizable numbers throughout most metropolitan areas.

Shopping goods, on the other hand, constitute seasonal to lifetime needs. They are of two kinds, fashion and service. The former consists of apparel and home furnishings. The latter includes a great many durable goods requiring installation and repair services, such as refrigerators, washing machines and automobiles. The department store is the key unit of the shopping goods stores.

Shopping goods cannot usually be ordered satisfactorily over the telephone. Customers are partially pulled from a given region by a wide variety of publicity media, which usually cover the entire metropolitan area. Thus, the congestion-locked central district stores often waste publicity dollars because they cannot handle trade from the entire area covered, due to changed transportation habits. A single outlying store

2. U. S. INCOME STUDY INDICATES INCREASED SALES

Standard of Living	1929 Income Level	% of Families	1949 Income Level	% of Families
Poverty—Bare Subsistence	Under $1699	42.2	Under $2399	30.0
Minimum Comfort, Comfort, Moderately Well-To-Do	$1700 to $5999	49.6	$2400 to $9499	66.0
Well-To-Do	$6000 and over	8.2	$9500 and over	4.0

Based on living standards estimated by Paul Nystrom of Columbia University in 1929, brought up to 1949 by Professor P. D. Converse of the University of Illinois, and further developed in Business Week

3. ALL FACTORS AFFECTING NUMBER AND TYPE OF EXPECTED CUSTOMERS ARE COMPUTED

Economic District (Toledo Area)	Time distance in minutes	Discount in % Time Dist.	Competition, existing habits GAF*	Competition, existing habits Food	Estimated No. of families 1949	Very Low	Low	Med.	High	Very High
City District #1	9	18%	75%	85%	14,600	14.5	24.9	46.2	13.1	1.2
85% Washington Township	10	19%	65%	75%	6,207	60.4	16.8	14.8	4.9	3.0
70% Adams Township	15	29%	70%	80%	3,133	60.4	16.8	14.8	4.9	3.0
City District #2	16	31%	85%	95%	18,108	38.5	26.3	25.0	8.2	2.0
Totals or Average					42,048	35.0	23.6	30.2	9.1	1.9

General merchandise, apparel and furniture stores

4. CONSERVATIVE ESTIMATE GIVES SALES POTENTIAL FOR PROPOSED SITE

Income Group	Annual Average Family Income	Annual Expenditure Per Family GAF	Annual Expenditure Per Family Food	Potential Annual Sales After Discounts GAF	Potential Annual Sales After Discounts Food
Very Low	$769*	$ 250	$ 536	$ 652,000	$ 801,000
Low	$2000	$ 575	$1000	$ 948,000	$ 874,000
Medium	$5500	$1130	$1450	$2,500,000	$1,765,000
High	over	$1950	$1900	$1,280,000	$ 688,000
Very High	$10,000	$2500	$2400	$ 362,000	$ 155,000
Totals				$5,742,000	$4,283,000

Part of expenditure is installment buying

without a central unit often cannot afford this kind of publicity. The shopping goods stores, therefore, form a logical nucleus for regional centers.

Existing Centers

In approaching a study for a new regional shopping center, one can learn much from an analysis of the advantages and disadvantages of existing facilities. The ideal regional shopping center combines the desirable qualities of both the downtown area and the more familiar types of present-day shopping centers.

The downtown center has, heretofore, been the only one providing an ample selection of shopping goods, and consequently has been the only real regional puller. It has also been a very logical centralization of vital activities of all kinds. The central district is generally at the hub of a mass transit system, and a system of thoroughfares and railroads which reach out into the surrounding metropolitan region. The large concentration of business and other activity attracts a great many people, labor force and visitors, creating in its relatively limited circulation area an economically useful, concentrated *pedestrian* purchasing power. In addition to this, the number of skilled retail operations and wide selection of merchandise augment the cumulative pull.

The extent of the region from which it pulls depends entirely upon the size and number of stores. The considerable investment in all kinds of commercial structures, and in effort in retailing, has created an anchor of tremendous importance to the community.

On the other hand, great difficulties have arisen in the downtown district because of the great confusion and interference of vehicles and pedestrians. Difficulty in moving goods in and out of the area has considerably increased costs of doing business. The limited street and parking areas cannot be economically increased to any appreciable extent in relation to floor area. Only if it were possible to do this could the central district be adapted to a greater use of automobiles for business and shopping needs. Additional parking in this limited area simply congests existing and economically frozen streets all the more. Even the mass transportation systems are proving inadequate to serve the fast-growing low density urban sprawl. Extension of these systems to any major degree would be difficult to support economically.

Concentrated pedestrian traffic in the downtown areas has also created "frontage values." Land values are often ten times as great as land only two or three blocks away. Collectively, its value is very much greater than any other area of the city. This has resulted in an im-

Both sites at right are in residential areas with good potential sales, ample highways. Stonestown Shopping Center, San Francisco, Calif. (near right), is planned as a balanced entity; Welton Becket, A.I.A., & Associates, Architects. Stores for R. H. Stearns Co. and S. S. Pierce Co., Boston, Mass. (plan and pond view, far right), flank a strip-like development; Walter Dorwin Teague, Designer

Moulin Studios Photo

portant assessed valuation, as well as a real value to the municipality in other respects. In many cases it has also resulted in as much as a third, or more, of the total property tax revenue for operating the central city. These values and revenues have been on a rapid decline, almost in direct ratio to the increased use of automobiles as a means of urban transportation. Revenues other than property taxes are increasingly logical and necessary to operate the central city, which must provide so many services and vital functions for the entire metropolitan area.

Many city planners, central district property owners and city officials claim that we must stop decentralization to preserve the tax-paying property values in the downtown area. They say it is necessary only to insure adequate off-street parking to do this. This is wishful thinking, in view of the economically and physically limited circulation and terminal areas available. Parking areas in most central districts have only 1/10 to 1/3 the amount of land used for buildings. In ideal suburban centers, parking must be three times the building area. Another school of thought recommends the creation of regional highways. Too often, this solution, alone, ends up in bringing greater amounts of traffic into the center, sometimes from a single direction, and does nothing to ease the inadequate terminal space. Combination of the two solutions would destroy the concentration of greatly varied commercial, governmental and cultural activities which are its life blood. The latest thinking in attempts to relieve congestion is to start with the traffic problem

where it is worst, in the center, and go outward in two or more directions. Then modern traffic engineering techniques, including a planned balance of thoroughfare capacity and intersection channelization, with communal parking facilities, can relieve the current paralyzing congestion.

Suburban shopping centers have sprung up in a great variety of types. The great majority of them have been primarily real estate developments, and have been initially successful because they have been able to take advantage of the dilemma of the downtown shopping area. Usually there has been no consideration of their effect on the overall transportation and economic pattern of the city.

Outlying centers have varied from the small cluster of a few convenience goods stores, to the larger neighborhood center, and finally the larger community center with 100 or more retail outlets. They are all products of antiquated zoning, often perpetuated by appeal boards not conversant with the comprehensive planning techniques so vitally needed in all central cities. The same confusion exists in the so-called "hot spot" shopping center as in the central district, but of a different degree. There is inadequate parking for shopping peaks, and there are few pedestrians on the streets. The vehicle traffic congestion is detrimental to the center, in addition to materially slowing down the inter-regional traffic, which must of necessity use these thoroughfares. The business thoroughfare or ribbon development has the same characteristics. When thoroughfares have been widened in an

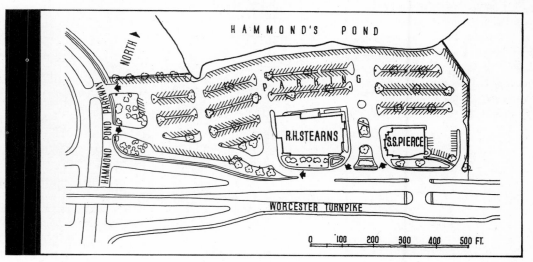

attempt to increase traffic flow capacity, they have often produced aggravated ribbons of commercial blight.

In spite of their shortcomings, these often uneconomic dispersals of thousands of stores are getting a considerable and increasing percentage of the total retail sales.

Many city-bound department stores have established branches in a variety of ways to meet the competition of these outlying shopping centers. Stores that carry fashion goods and those carrying a great variety of items, such as an outlet of a large mail order chain, have built many isolated branch units in outlying areas. The site selected is often a part of, or close to, a "proven location." These are usually on thoroughfares which become inadequate and congested with the addition of such an extra traffic generator. Most provided a fair amount of parking space initially, but not enough for present day needs.

Many of these isolated branches have ended up as part of a strip real estate promotion. Neglect of the fundamentals of modern shopping has considerably limited their effectiveness and sales productivity. They often present too small a selection of goods to be truly representative of the parent store. The cumulative pull created by having competitors in the same field conveniently adjacent to each other is often ignored.

Another solution, tried by a great many large department stores, has been to build a branch store in the existing retail district of a suburban town. This is generally on high-cost land, and has many of the same basic drawbacks as the downtown area of the central city in the light of the transportation trends of today.

The out-of-the-center mail order retail outlet has usually been an individual success. This is generally because of its size, distributive skill, the great variety of stock carried, and the fact that it has had the mail order technique to fall back on. It has also generally provided generous parking facilities.

Most of these branches have been successful, even if they haven't realized their full sales potential. Studies that have been made to determine if a branch took sales from the downtown store have shown that, if anything, sales were probably helped. Interest created in the stores has brought a percentage of customers to the central units for a wider selection of high-cost fashion and durable goods. The economic shock of too many branches opening in a short period can initially harm total central sales, but in time a healthy balance should be restored.

Thus, with a continued metropolitan growth, the large downtown stores that acquire suburban branches on the right pattern, have a good chance, after initial adjustments, of maintaining downtown sales at present relative levels, and at the same time increase sales over the entire metropolitan area from 50 to 100 per cent.

The Ideal Solution

The design of a new regional type of center must be long-range planning in its best sense, and fit into a logical economic pattern for the entire metropolitan area. It should not be treated solely as a real estate

STORE BUILDING
SOLID WALL
GLASS WALL
COVERED PEDESTRIAN WAY
LANDSCAP'G
PARKING (6 CARS)
+ TRAFFIC LIGHT

GROSS GROUND COVERAGE AREAS

A 11,200 SQ. FT.
B 5,200 " "
C 18,800 " "
D 14,000 " "
E 15,000 " "
F 4,000 " "
G 22,800 " "
H 8,000 " "

99,000 TOTAL SQ. FT.

EMPLOYEES PARKING

BUS STA

NORTH

Table 5 (right) estimates possible areas for Toledo Center, derived from potential sales in Table 4. Proportionate pull of stores was considered in allotting areas. Plan gives more concrete solution for actual site. Buildings are indicated as follows: A—food store; B—drugstore; part of C—convenience goods; rest of C, D, E, F—shopping goods; G—department store; H—restaurant; building indicated at top right is a service station

development, but rather as the integrated team work of planners, architects, engineers, store and property managers, financial institutions and real estate organizations.

Taking into consideration the assets and deficiencies of existing retail districts and branches, the formula for an ideal center would include all of the following seven factors:

1. *The location* of a regional shopping center should be based on a realistic, conservative economic study of an area. One approach in selecting a site is shown in the analysis of the Toledo, Ohio, area made for the Sylvania-Douglas Realty Co. by the Grand Rapids Store Equipment Co. (page 170). This method is to analyze a given region within 20 to 45 minutes time distance, as to extent of population, family incomes, and for what goods money is spent. Family expenditure for basic food and clothing can vary considerably with communities of different character. Potential growth and changes in demands should also be considered in this analysis.

Next a discount or allowance should be applied for the time distance it takes these varying kinds of customers to reach the center. Successive discounts should also be made to compensate for competition from existing or projected centers, including the central business district, and the relative ease of reaching it by transportation facilities. The discount for time distance can be based on 20 to 45 minutes equaling 100 per cent, depending on the kind and scope of merchandise pre-

sented, and is usually figured to vary from 12 to 98 per cent. This is based on the simple reasoning that the further away in time distance, or the more inconvenient it is to reach a given center as compared with other groups, the less frequently will visits be made. The time distance allowance considers the types of streets and thoroughfares which can serve the center. A driver will travel three times the distance in a given time period on an expressway, as compared to the congested traffic signal-ridden street. Under certain circumstances, when the maximum discounts for both factors are superimposed one upon the other, it results in a virtual cancellation of an area as far as the computation of potential sales is concerned.

These studies will determine the number of potential customers which can be expected at a prospective site. Expenditures will vary as to type and amount in different income levels. Multiplied by the averages of these annual expenditures, the number of expected customers gives the sales potential of the site. The proper size of the center is derived from this potential as shown in Table 5 above. An extensive study will give the number of such centers which, in a series, can completely blanket and serve an entire metropolitan area.

After deciding on an area with good potential sales, it is necessary to consider the topographical situation, zoning restrictions and the availability of necessary thoroughfares, services, and utilities. To create economically all of the desired advantages in a center, low cost acreage for the site is essential. In general, the fur-

5. GROSS AREAS OF STORES ARE DERIVED FROM SALES POTENTIAL.

Type of Store or Area	Gross Area Sq Ft	Avg. Annual Sales per Gross Sq Ft	Sales Avg. Productivity	Sales Avg. High Productivity
Department Store	45,600	55	$2,500,000	$3,300,000
Apparel and Home Furnishings Stores, Variety Stores	37,500	40	1,500,000	1,800,000
Total G A F Sales	83,100	49	4,000,000	5,100,000
Misc. Stores, Shops, Drug Stores	22,200	45	1,000,000	1,220,000
Food Stores, Restaurants	19,700	76	1,500,000	1,770,000
Services	8,000			
Total	133,000*		$6,500,000	$8,090,000
Building Ground Coverage	100,000			
Parking Area, access roads	527,000			
Landscaping, Misc.	158,000			
Total Ground Area	785,000			

About 75 per cent of gross area would be entering level.

A built-up district requires near-total site coverage by building. Wolf Wile Co., Lexington, Ky.; Frankel & Curtis, Architects; Amos Parrish & Co., Designers

ther out the center is, and the more unused land there is adjacent to the site, the easier it is to control traffic and surroundings. Immediate surroundings are best if undeveloped and suitable for sound residential building.

It is also advisable to see what possible mass transportation can serve the center for the convenience of a part of the customers, and for the labor force. A high percentage of employees do not use private automobiles for transportation. However, there are a great many potential employees who live in the suburbs and form a logical labor market, especially for part-time work.

2. *Highway and thoroughfare* congestion in reaching the center should be positively eliminated. Convenience and safety require not only added highway capacity, but ample dispersal, and reservoir space for channeling vehicles to eliminate left turns across traffic.

There are few if any existing street capacities or patterns in built-up areas that can serve the great amount of parking necessary to handle the December sales peak of shopping goods stores. Most major thoroughfares or main streets that serve regional traffic are already congested, without imposing on them the burden of an additional traffic generator. Even on so-called regional highways, the closer you get to the center of the city, the greater is the traffic and congestion.

One or more limited access highways provide the best kind of thoroughfares for this purpose. They should be ample, fast, safe and uncongested, and should have a capacity in excess of current demands. Many centers have donated some of the land for widening streets to

create such thoroughfares. Arrangements can often be made with highways authorities for the proper facilities, as they are of mutual benefit to the center and the residents of surrounding areas.

Perhaps the easiest way to eliminate traffic congestion is to place the regional center well away from densely built-up areas with concentrated traffic. This is contrary to much current thinking on the location of centers, and would not work except for the definite and thoroughly proven cumulative pull of a planned group of well established stores.

3. *A balanced group of stores* should be included as to type, number and size, to create a maximum cumulative pull, as worked out in the chart shown above. The majority should be branches of key, well established downtown department and specialty stores. Full advantage should be taken of the stores' merchandising skill, wide publicity, and good will. People are attracted to a center by what they know they can find there in the way of goods and services, and by what they read is there in the papers, or see or hear on the air. The store signs, and even display windows, as seen by passers-by, are relatively minor factors in total year in and year out sales.

The larger stores should be competitive. Maximum pulling power and productivity have always been produced by healthy competition. Better fashion goods merchants thrive on such a situation, however they should not have to compete in the real estate business as well. In addition, certain variety and drug chains

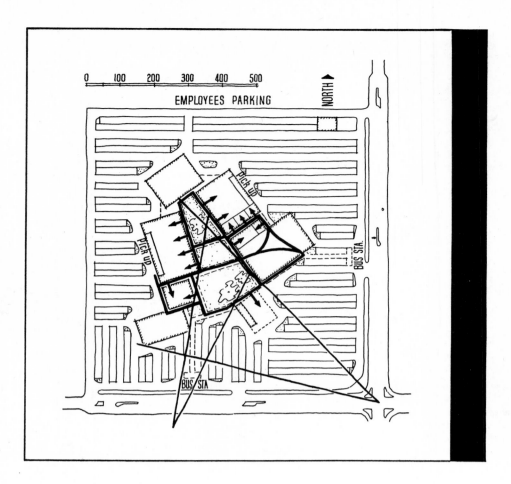

Plot layout (right) of the Toledo center separates peripheral parking from pedestrian ways in mall. Buildings are disposed for maximum visibility into store fronts from highways (medium lines on plan). Department store is located for maximum impact; food store and restaurant for roadside publicity. Pedestrian ways (dark lines) are covered, as are walks to bus stops

should be represented to the extent they satisfy a demand and help sales for the entire center. In effect, the center should be a miniature "downtown," and closely allied with it. The exact size depends on the estimated potential sales.

A minor area could be devoted to convenience goods stores, including a supermarket. There should also be other stores, including a good restaurant. A combination movie house and theater for fashion shows and goods demonstrations can be an asset. However, current controls and the impact of television on neighborhood theaters make it difficult to obtain a satisfactory lease. There would be a balanced selection of "homemaking" services and, if needed, some professional offices for the convenience of suburbanites.

The branches of existing stores should be of sufficient size to reflect the prestige of the parent stores. Density pattern in the community, and existing mass transit systems also govern size. Space for relative sales, selling facilities and potential forward stocks must be carefully compared with those in the main store. Merchandise should be selected in a given number of price ranges that established customers expect to find. Total quantity is reduced, but normal demands should be fully met. This also allows regional publicity to apply to both branch and parent store.

Provision for reserve stocks in the store, and for their distribution from a central warehouse, must also be studied to take care of large "take withs" due to peak sales periods and convenient parking. This can reduce delivery expense ratios up to 75 per cent. For this, different layouts and types of equipment are needed from that of the downtown store.

In general, the larger store has personnel and organizational advantages which attract greater managerial skill. Such branch stores, as part of a planned center, create important "anchors" as far as site location and buying habits are concerned.

4. *The plot layout* should be completely geared to the convenient and safe use of automobiles. Ample parking should be allotted to handle the December peak. Most well planned centers today consider the minimum satisfactory ratio of parking space to net selling space to be 3 to 1. Much more is preferable. The maintenance of this ratio should be written into the lease. This is only possible on large undeveloped tracts, not on narrow strips created by streetcar patterns.

Parking lanes should be two-way, and have 90 degrees parking. The latter accommodates more cars per sq ft and gives shorter walking distances. A peripheral road is needed around the center to give access to parking spaces. Private vehicle traffic near the stores should be discouraged in plan.

The parking turnover (number of cars parked in a day, divided by car spaces available) often averages only once per day on a yearly basis for branch department stores. For convenience goods stores, it can be ten times or more. This is due to the fact that one can buy a week's supply of food in 20 minutes or so, while it sometimes takes several hours to select fashion goods.

Richard Garrison Photo

Upper left: parking for R. H. Stearns and S. S. Pierce branches is separated from adjacent stores by troublesome fence. Lower left: 6-acre site for Woodward & Lothrop store, Chevy Chase, Md., is to be expanded by 3 acres to handle parking; Starrett and Van Vleck, Architects. Above: Wolf Wile Co. has only side street for parking

In smaller centers, from the merchandising viewpoint, it is important to decide at the outset how much of the parking is to be in front and how much in back. The entrance adjacent to the largest parking area becomes the "front" for all practical purposes. Parking areas can sometimes be enlarged by use of double-deck parking, basements, or roofs.

It is generally bad planning to try to limit a parking area to the use of a single store of a shopping group. Customers usually shop or make purchases at a number of the stores. Any store creates ill will if it tries to limit a lot to its exclusive use.

There should be minimum walking distances between parked cars and covered walks, and between stores. This often becomes a problem if the center is too large or dispersed. There should also be a completely separated pedestrian way adjacent to the store frontage, reached by covered arcades in the parking areas. Highway traffic and parking areas should be carefully concealed from the pedestrian shopper. Besides giving better vistas from inside the shops and along the walks, it produces a concentration of pedestrian traffic, promoting greater impulse sales. It also gives a separation of pedestrians from moving vehicles, adding to convenience and safety.

Loading areas for incoming and outgoing goods should be placed for minimum interference with pedestrian and private vehicle traffic. The use of costly truck tunnels for this purpose is currently a matter of some controversy. A system of pick-up stations, with or without conveyors, will encourage shoppers to take purchases with them, thus materially lowering delivery costs.

5. *The design and plans of the buildings* should be well integrated with the site plan, and present merchandise in the best manner possible to the planned, concentrated pedestrian traffic. It must be economical, convenient, spacious and in good taste. The architectural impact from the highway should also be considered; about 90 per cent of the shoppers can be expected to arrive by automobile.

A mall scheme layout of the buildings, as shown in the plan above, has the advantage, compared with an on-the-street center, of having two rows of stores facing each other. With this plan, there is no "best" side of the street, and all stores are within convenient walking distance. Concentration of pedestrians on the inner loop considerably increases impulse buying. Secondary axes used to "avoid the monotony," and without any real merchandising function, do little but create dead "side streets." Large centers might have a center mall with two levels of covered sidewalks and store fronts. A good example of this type is the new Middlesex Center, now under construction near Boston, Mass., designed by Morris Ketchum. This device eliminates the necessity for any basement selling areas, usually a drug on the market in suburban centers. Suburban branches do not as a rule carry bargain basement type merchandise.

Arcades leading to the interior mall should be featured architecturally. Walks in the mall itself should

Studies should consider a center's impact on motorists and pedestrians. The sketches (right) for the Toledo center show these two points of view. Merchandise, rather than flamboyant architecture, is emphasized by simple open fronts. The motorist's view is led into landscaped mall; pedestrians are screened from parking areas

be covered. Open fronts are desirable for the stores, with treatment centered on the interior designs to create more impulse buying. Objectionable daylight reflections should be carefully controlled. Open fronts and covered walks eliminate much of the expense of competitive facades. They also permit a more unified planning of the group, while still maintaining ample individuality of appearance. A standardized, simplified structural system can materially reduce costs. With modern lighting and ventilating techniques, ceiling heights can be kept to a minimum. This reduces cubage and the expense of elevators and moving stairways. The design should provide for future reallocation of space, and for flexible store equipment which can be reused and interchanged, even between stores. If future expansion is planned for any of the stores, foundations and structures designed for the addition of extra floors will prevent encroachment on land areas reserved for parking. Otherwise, adjacent property must be available to preserve the recommended minimum 3 to 1 parking area to building ratio.

Signs should be orderly, and designed to be seen from high speed highways. Signs should be included for the center as a whole, and for the larger key pullers. The key restaurant, often an important puller, can have a special identity, easily seen from the highways, because it has to remain open when other stores and services are closed.

6. *The area surrounding* the center must be controlled for the benefit of the community as a whole, as well as for the developers and merchants of the center. It should be built up in a constructive manner with permanent zone protection, or be under complete control of the shopping center ownership. When the surrounding area is owned by the developer, control can be obtained through voluntary zoning or through deed restriction, to produce a useful surrounding residential area. Agreements should be made with the civil or local government on taxes.

The ideal site design inherently provides a protective buffer for the surrounding residential area. This protects the investment from detrimental commercial encroachment, which generally produces uncontrollable congestion. The ideal pattern, with a large amount of parking and open landscaped spaces, provides maximum protection for the entire area.

7. *The management* of the center must be merchandise minded, and interested in long range investment, not quick turnover. It must give every possible aid in furthering increased productivity of space, and consider itself a partner of the retailer, not a landlord in the usual sense. Full cooperation must exist on all matters pertaining to opening hours, publicity, services, credit and the like.

The management must assume a great many operating and maintenance problems to reduce their cost and to permit the retailer to fully concentrate on his merchandise selling job. Efficient central heat and cooled

Large glazed areas permit landscaped vistas in suburbs, as in S. S. Pierce branch (inset, upper left). In built-up areas, as Wolf Wile Co. (above), glazing still permits view of goods inside shops

water for air conditioning should be sold to each store on a metered basis. Ventilating and lighting equipment can be purchased by the tenant for amortization, timing and tax purposes.

If the center is kept open two or more evenings a week, greatly increased sales generally result. Two of the most important factors in assuring success are regional advertising and proven good will. These can be best accomplished by close team work of the merchants and management.

The Intermediate Solution

Often in medium to smaller metropolitan areas all the elements of the ideal center are not available. Sometimes, however, a fortunate circumstance has provided enough undeveloped land, with a rectangular rather than too elongated shape, that can be used to advantage. It is generally well within a built up outlying section of the city, or in a suburb or separate civil division, that has a concentration of medium to high income-group residential areas within a relatively small radius of, say, 15 to 20 minutes. Such a property can often be found in one parcel, with a single ownership. To protect the investment, the merchant should be assured by agreement throughout the length of the lease and its extensions, that physical and economic principles will be maintained.

Other basic principles of the large center should also be applied. They include:

1. The maintenance of a definite ratio between parking spaces and usable structural area.

2. Balance of compatible stores. If the center is small and can support only a few stores, they should be all of one kind. These should be shopping goods stores, not convenience goods, except perhaps for a restaurant. This will create a maximum cumulative pull of a given kind. Customers on weekly shopping trips for food seldom shop for fashion apparel and vice versa. A collection of established fashion stores, since they are relatively few and far between, will pull from a greater time distance if there is ample parking.

3. Location is best on a not too heavily traveled thoroughfare, where the center is the only important traffic generator. This requires that it be made up of well known and continually publicized stores.

4. Control of surrounding areas is usually not as important as with larger centers, for built-up areas of the character described usually have protective zoning. However, some control, if even ownership of scattered lots or parcels, is insurance against future destructive and often politically inspired zoning changes. The problems are more often to get such a tract zoned commercial, and to cope with obsolete building codes and restrictions on the style of the structures. These can often be overcome by proving that the center will provide a useful additional economic and tax base for the community without harming — but rather helping — existing business in the area.

STONESTOWN SHOPPING

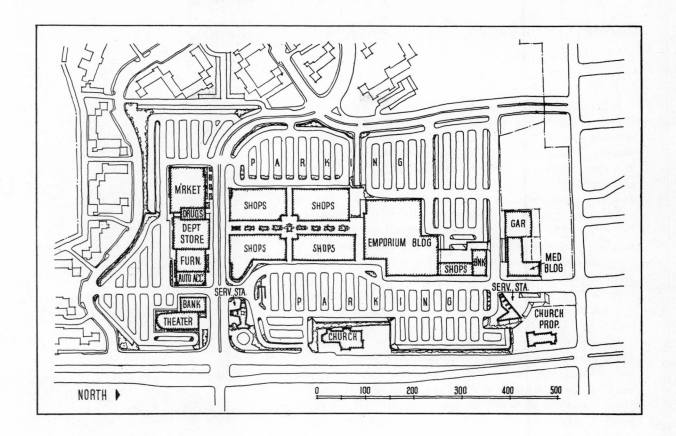

CENTER, SAN FRANCISCO, CALIF.

Welton Becket, A.I.A., & Associates, Architects

Disposition of buildings around the central mall is shown in the plan (above) and two large photos (left). This scheme serves to separate pedestrian and traffic flow, as indicated on chart below. The inset (far left) superimposes the project model on a photograph of its site

THIS LARGE, CAREFULLY PLANNED SHOPPING CENTER in San Francisco's Lakeside district typifies the regional type of center discussed in the preceding article. A 35 acre site adjoining Stonestown, an extensive apartment development, was selected for the center by Harry and Ellis Stoneson, owners and builders of the project. The area is served by ample thoroughfares. It is bounded by a golf course, the San Francisco State College campus, and residential sections, all of which will serve to protect the center against uncontrolled commercial encroachment. The mall and two buildings for the center are under construction — a branch for the Emporium department store and a medical center.

A year of study and analysis of the area was spent before actual designing of the center was begun. Potential sales were estimated at $48,000,000 per year, to approximately 400,000 people in the surrounding regions. On the basis of these figures, the size of the development was practically doubled as compared with the first concept. An analysis to determine size and number of outlets, indicated, among other things, that drugstores were below par in area, and that a theater should have a capacity of 1800 instead of smaller as originally planned.

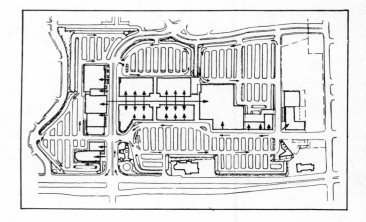

With the Emporium branch as the key store, the center will include a mall with speciality shops, and a secondary department store group. Commercial goods stores will include two super markets, drugstores, service stations, a restaurant, and such services as barber shops and repair shops. There will also be an office building, two banks, the theater and the medical building.

Parking is provided for 3000 cars in peripheral parking areas and several enclosed garages. Stores will be serviced from a subterranean street. The stores are disposed around a central mall axis to concentrate pedestrian shopping. Most of the shops also have street entrances. The location of each shop has been studied in relation to major units, its ability to attract customers, and to parking.

Designs of the various buildings have been coordinated into a unified whole, with the major department store dominating. They will be constructed of fieldstone, brick, concrete and glass. The structure of the Emporium store is designed to accommodate future expansion. The entire site will be landscaped to preserve the suburban setting.

Leases for the shops will be on a percentage basis, and will specify the types of signs that can be used.

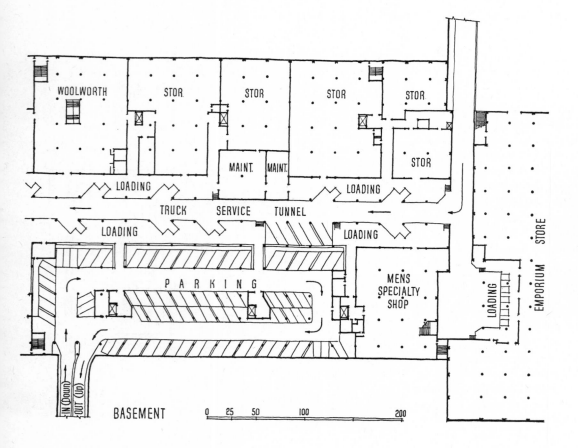

BASEMENT

The dominant building of the center (left and below) is the branch of the Emporium department store, now under construction. It will carry a complete stock of shopping goods to create a major sales pull in the region. Competitive shops and stores will flank it to present a wide choice of goods to the shopper. Convenience goods stores and professional services terminate the group at either end. Loading facilities for the stores and parking garages are located beneath the central group (plan, far left). The service drive for trucks is visible in the lower right portions of the photos at left and below center

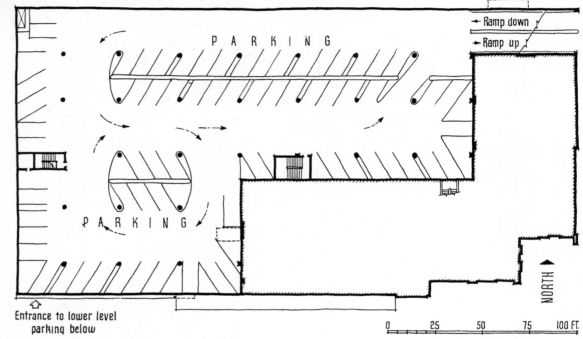

Ramp down
Ramp up

PARKING

PARKING

NORTH

The final rendering of the medical center is shown above. Top floors of the L-shaped structure will house professional suites for doctors. The ground floor will include a bank, post office, pharmacy and 8 specialty stores. A two-level garage will flank the building (plan, left), and provide parking for 125 cars. Photo below shows theater (left), service station (center)

Entrance to lower level parking below

0   25   50   75   100 FT.

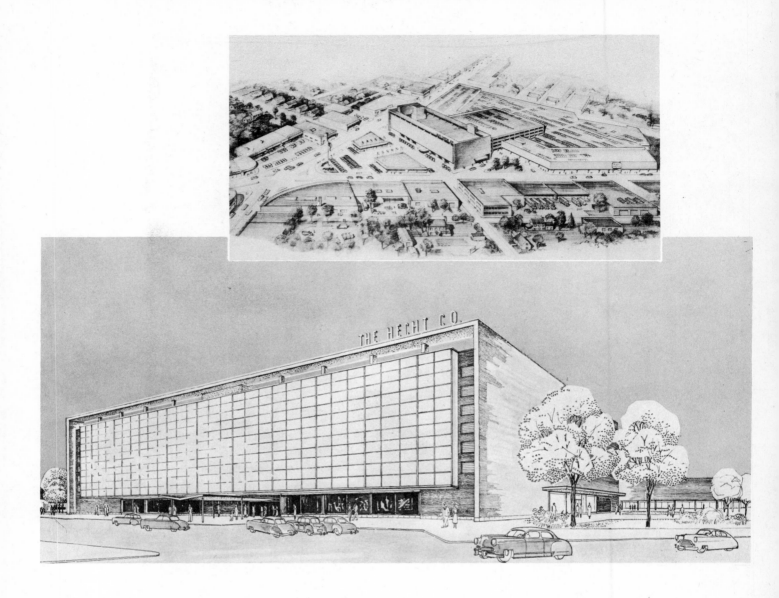

SHOPPING CENTER FOR THE HECHT CO.

Abbott, Merkt & Co., Architects and Engineers

Kahn and Jacobs, Consulting Architects

THE TREMENDOUS VALUE OF COMPETITION in promoting sales led The Hecht Co., a Washington, D. C., department store, to develop a 41-store shopping center in nearby Virginia. Most of the stores will sell merchandise in direct competition to the department store branch. The project is now under construction.

The center is located on an 18 acre, triangular plot, at the intersection of three major thoroughfares. Plans call for widening two of the roads to six lanes, one to five lanes. The Hecht Co. has dedicated the necessary land adjoining the center. Population of surrounding counties has increased 124 per cent in the past decade.

The high average family income in the area is estimated to give large potential sales.

In addition to shopping goods stores, the center will include supermarkets, drug, hardware and specialty food stores. There will also be a bank, postoffice, Western Union, and automobile showrooms. Shops will be built to specifications of the tenants, but in conformity to the overall architectural design.

The shape, and rather limited size of the plot led to the use of roof parking, with a four-tiered garage over the central area. A 90 ft wide promenade separates The Hecht store from the rest of the center.

Parking areas on the roof and in the parking garage (above) will accommodate 2500 cars at one time. It is estimated that this will handle 10,000 cars a day at the normal rate of turnover. Passageways will connect each floor of the parking garage to corresponding floors of The Hecht Co. store. Loading and receiving platforms will be located underground so that trucks making deliveries will not conflict with customer parking. The promenade between the department store and the other shops (below) will afford protection from sun and rain, and lead past the various display windows. Other landscaped pedestrian walks will surround the center

Richard Averill Smith, Photo

IN CONTRAST TO THE COMPLETE CENTERS presented on the previous pages, these branch stores for S. S. Pierce Co. and R. H. Stearns are separately conceived and managed units adjoining the Chestnut Hill Shopping Center, near Boston, Mass. The entire strip-like center includes two other privately built stores and a small group of developer-sponsored shops. The site (see plan, page 173) is located in a pleasant suburban setting between Hammond's Pond and the Worcester Turnpike. Good potential sales were indicated by the higher income group in the area, many of which are clients of the parent stores, and by the proximity of an apartment development across the turnpike. This highway is to be depressed in front of the center in the near future, with

TWO STORES FOR BOSTON, MASS.

Walter Dorwin Teague, Designer

Robert J. Harper and Carl R. Conrad, Associates

Edward A. Ashley, Engineer

Morton C. Tuttle Co., Builders

Richard Averill Smith, Photo

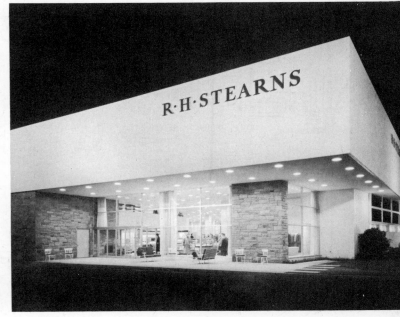

adjacent service roads leading to the stores. Little effect is expected from this change, as the two stores don't depend greatly on impulse buying, due to the price range and nature of the goods: S. S. Pierce Co. sells specialty foods, R. H. Stearns is a department store featuring fashion goods and some housewares.

The two stores, planned jointly, share a 550-car parking area.

The exteriors of the stores employ sun louvers, baffles and overhangs as architectural features on the southern sides, to reduce glare and reflection on window areas. Extensive use is made of night lighting (photos, right). The structure of the Stearns branch is designed for expansion to double the original floor area. Interiors of both shops are planned to take advantage of lake and suburban views.

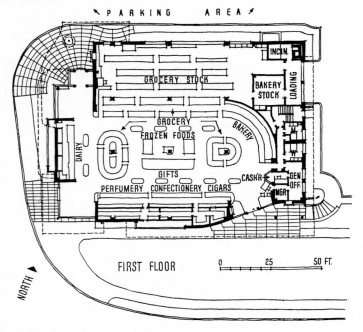

The plan for the S. S. Pierce Co. branch (above) affords two "fronts" for the building—one for the parking area to the north, one for the highway on the south (right). Loading is removed to one side

R. H. Stearns (below) is planned to look like a specialty shop. Departments for children, men and housewares are concealed from main sales area. Stock and fitting rooms are scattered for convenience. Related accessories are grouped together to facilitate sales

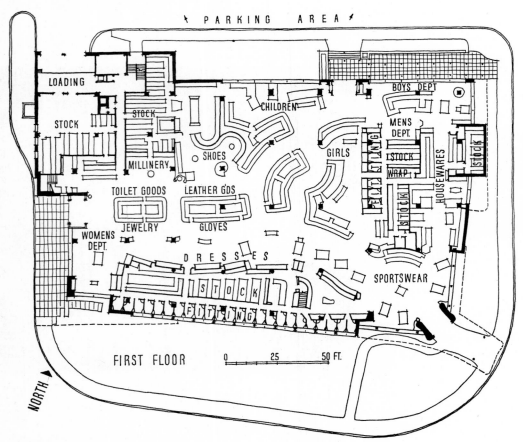

The interior of S. S. Pierce Co. (above) is planned for maximum display of the maroon-labeled goods. Color and lighting are used for decorative effects, glazed areas give vistas of lake

Richard Averill Smith Photos

The north facade of R. H. Stearns (above) has large glazed areas, protective canopies for entrance. Street entrance (above right) overlooks tree-lined street, as does the women's department at right

March 1951

STORE FOR WOODWARD & LOTHROP

Chevy Chase, Maryland   *Starrett and Van Vleck, Architects*

FOLLOWING THE TREND of decentralization, Woodward & Lothrop, a conservative Washington, D. C., department store, has established this branch in Chevy Chase, Md., where a good portion of its clients reside. Although it is a single outlying store, many of the principles of the ideal shopping center have been applied. The size of the branch was carefully studied so that it would adequately represent the wide range of goods offered by the parent store. Regional publicity can thus be effectively used by both stores. The original 6 acre site, located at the intersection of three avenues, provided parking for 500 cars. Three additional acres to the west recently have been purchased to accommodate 400 more cars. The parking spaces radiate from the building to lessen walking distances. The rear entrance to the building is at basement level, the other two at the first floor. Loading areas are completely separated from other activities.

STORE FOR JOHN WANAMAKER

Wilmington, Delaware   *Massena & duPont, Architects*

THE EFFECT OF THE AUTOMOBILE has also been felt in the location of new stores in smaller cities. Typical of this is a new store (right) for John Wanamaker's, which has stores in several cities. It has been built a mile from the heart of downtown Wilmington, Del. By such a move, the firm was able to obtain space for parking, and to assure easy access to the store via an adjacent thoroughfare cutoff.

Besides the usual department store services, the new unit provides a bank, first aid center and an auditorium. The building is on sloping ground, which permits entry at the second floor at the rear, at the first floor in the front. Moving stairs and elevators join the various levels. Entrance driveways and walkways surrounding the store are equipped with an underground snow melting system to encourage shopping during the colder months.

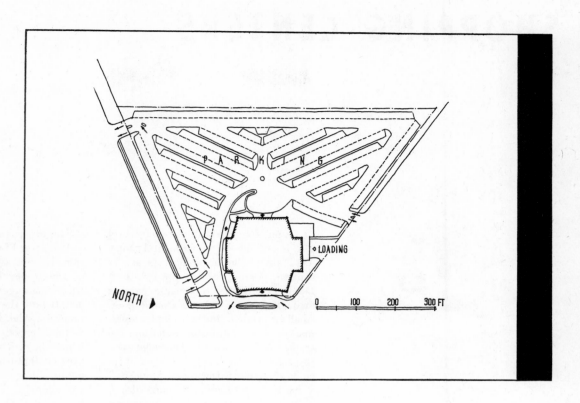

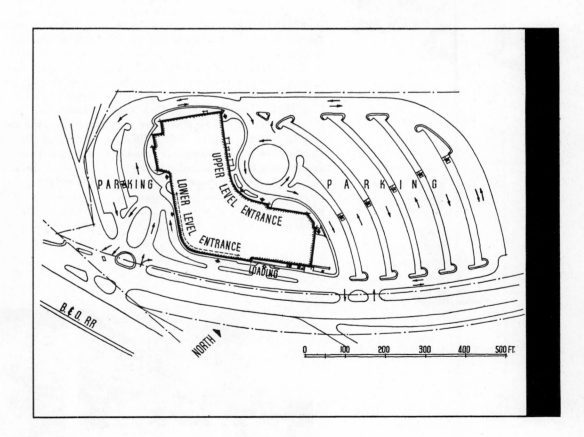

SHOPPING CENTERS

As a building type the shopping center is still in· the experimental stage. Yet it already has inspired a typical conception: a group of one- or two-story buildings adjacent to a large parking area. The stores on the ground floor, small and varied, cluster around a supermarket and a drugstore, sharing the traffic which these can be depended upon to promote. The bigger centers will include also a movie theater, a "5 and 10," a bank, a restaurant, perhaps also a branch department store. On the second floor (if there is one) will be offices for doctors, dentists, lawyers, and other professional men.

This group of stores and offices will often be somewhat withdrawn from the highway; they may even turn their backs upon it, as though spurning the automobile which jogged them into existence (although they will pamper the automobile which comes bearing customers — the recommended ratio of parking space to store space becomes larger every year).

In 1925 automobiles in the U. S. ran up 200 billion passenger miles, more or less. In 1940 the figure was 500 billion. Combine these facts with the depression and the urge to lower distribution costs, and you have the cash-and-carry supermarket, which the average housewife visits three times a week, taking the goods home in her car.

The bus has replaced the trolley car as the favored form of urban transportation. In contrast to the rigid armature of the trolley lines with their costly tracks, bus routes can be quickly changed, adapted to the creation of new communities. And whereas the trolley car certainly encouraged strip development, it may be claimed that the bus encourages satellite towns (just as the private automobile gives birth to the independent shopping centers isolated except from roads). The satellite towns in their turn encourage the planned neighborhood shopping center which has now come to be considered an essential amenity in all large new housing developments — particularly since developers have come to realize what profits may lie in store leasing.

The more widespread and obvious result of the automobile's popularity is the ring of inchoate suburbs which already scatter out like a shot pattern from all large towns, in exploitation of lower-cost land. This is typical shopping center and branch department store territory, the lower land cost justifying sprawling one- or two-story buildings and large parking areas.

Use of the automobile, however, by the suddenness of its growth, has set increasingly restricted limits on its own usefulness. Its convenience depends less upon distance than upon traffic con-

By Bruno Funaro and Geoffrey Baker

This study is based on the research of Bruno Funaro, A.I.A., as McKim Fellow, Columbia University, 1948–49. It has been

prepared by Bruno Funaro and Geoffrey Baker who are at present collaborating on a book covering the same subject

gestion. The trading area of any store group has changed not only in scale but in shape also. It is no longer a simple circle of so many miles radius. Based on driving time it becomes an irregular cookie shape. In most of the ambitious shopping centers now in the planning stage, considerable importance is given to a site easily accessible from a number of major, fast-traffic highways.

Side by side with the plans which depend mainly upon automobile traffic are others based on the traffic promoted by an existing transportation center such as a railroad station or long-distance bus terminal (with, however, a great deal of parking space added to serve those arriving in their own cars). Many plans have also been drawn for making the existing downtown shopping areas more attractive by the provision of extra parking space. Because of the number of vested interests involved, such schemes probably will remain pigeonholed for many years to come, except in some smaller towns where the investments are not so large, the pressure against change less strong (see pages 196, 197).

All types of shopping center envisage a certain amount of control, which is normally enforced by all the stores being in one ownership. Each store depends upon the landlord to see that he is subjected to no more than the small amount of fair competition which attracts the customer. This, combined with the proximity of traffic-getters such as supermarkets and department stores, makes location in a shopping center particularly attractive to the small merchant. In return for a slightly higher rent (for he is subsidizing the traffic-getters) he is guaranteed traffic, prestige, and a certain stability which Main Street cannot always provide.

Every privately promoted shopping center will have profit as its *raison d'être*, just as every store which rents space will have to be convinced that it is a good spot to make a profit. So, in order to sell his tenants, and perhaps convince himself too, the promoter must build up a statistical picture of his prospective customers.

He will want to know how much *Buying Power* this new center may hope to tap. First he must decide the total income of the area from which it is hoped to draw trade. Yardsticks commonly used are distribution of income-tax returns and non-commercial telephones, proportion of homeowners to non-homeowners, number of servants, etc. To discover the *net* Buying Power, subtract from this total income all that is already committed to others — e.g., rent to the landlord, and business already going to existing stores. All this figuring is clouded by almost endless assumptions and shading. For example, it is usually necessary to work with 1940 census figures (in most cases the latest available), and these can usually be brought up to date only after many modifications, which depend for their correctness on hunch and experience. Finally the 1940 figures, and any others used, must be corrected by means of the Cost of Living Index to allow for changed dollar values.

The next step is to make a survey of *existing stores:* type, quality, sales volume, convenience (location, and amenities such as parking).

Next it is necessary to calculate a *radius of attraction.* This will be based on such considerations as driving time, public transportation, walking distance, shopping habits, etc.

From these facts the promoter will be able to judge what form his center should take and where it should be placed. He should be able to judge what type of stores will be most successful there, how many, how large; and what other types of enterprises should be included — a theater perhaps, a restaurant, offices. And the nature of his tenants will give him some idea of the turnover to expect in the parking area, which in turn will govern its size. And if he is wise he will remember also (even if he doesn't admit it) that all these elaborate calculations can be thrown out of balance by some rival promoter starting another center nearby.

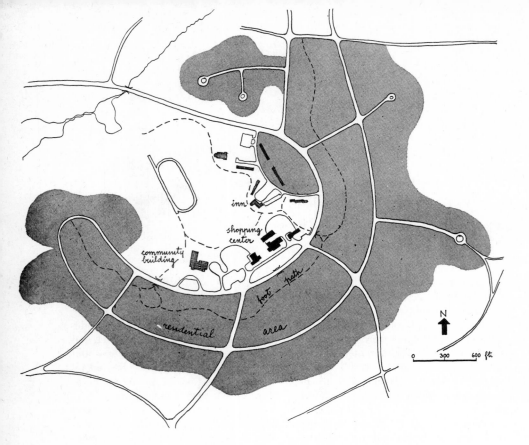

Left:
Hemmed in on three sides by residential zones, with a community recreation park completing the encirclement, the store group in Greenbelt, Md. (built by the Resettlement Administration, 1936) makes no attempt to attract custom from those outside the community. But it is at the center of a convergent pattern of roads and footpaths (with underpasses) which help to channel the shopping habits of those within the community

Right:
A neighborhood center, serving some 2000 families, this modern version of the traditional village green includes a swimming pool, a children's playground, and a community building with restaurant and bowling alleys, in addition to a row of stores. Embedded in the middle of a residential community, a center such as this does not expect to draw passing trade from a main highway. Levittown, Long Island, N. Y., developed by Levitt & Sons

The suitability of any site for a shopping center should be judged under three main heads:

Accessibility—by private car, by public transportation (bus, trolley car, subway), on foot from nearby houses.

Zoning—of the site itself and of adjacent property.

Topography—the shape, size, contours and physical features of the plot.

ACCESSIBILITY

Shoppers will arrive on foot, by private car, and by public transportation. Except in densely populated areas foot traffic is of small importance in the total traffic which any center can hope to attract. Local conditions, such as distance from residential and business areas, preformed habits, the type of stores included in the shopping center, and the

wealth of prospective customers, all influence the manner in which these reach the new group of stores.

In deciding the site itself and the position of stores on that site, the aim should always be to make it as easy as possible for customers to reach these stores, bearing in mind local shopping habits. For example, stores on one side of a major thoroughfare might seem to

Alongside a main highway, this shopping center (not yet completed) at College Park, Md., includes a separate restaurant, right on the road, to pull in long-distance travelers. The plan of this center is typical of the L-shaped type with front parking which has already proved successful in the Washington area. This one has some additional roof parking (see page 200). Architects: Berla & Abel

Funneling pedestrian traffic through a central arcade between a large group of two-story apartments (Foster Village) and a main road bus station, this group of stores at Bergenfield, N. J., with its large area of front parking, should also attract shoppers coming in automobiles from neighboring communities. The curve of the building increases store frontage and encourages window shopping. Architect: Alan Wood Fraser

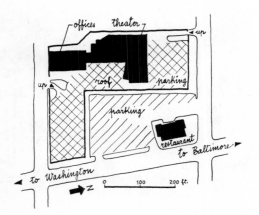

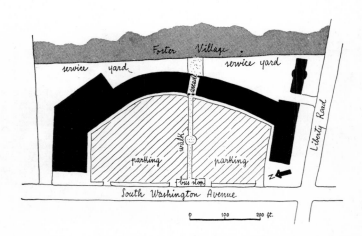

Thomas Airviews Photo

local customers much more easily reached (and therefore more popular) than competing stores almost directly opposite. Location near a commuter railroad station, near a bus stop or a subway station, may become an important factor in the success of a new center. Anything that promotes traffic is popular with a majority of the smaller store owners.

In addition to the local shoppers there are the long-distance automobile travelers who want to stop for a meal, or to fill up at a gas station. They may also be induced to do some impulse buying at an adjacent group of stores. Traffic counts can give some inkling of what such trade could amount to, but other factors, such as the side of the highway on which the stores are placed, and their

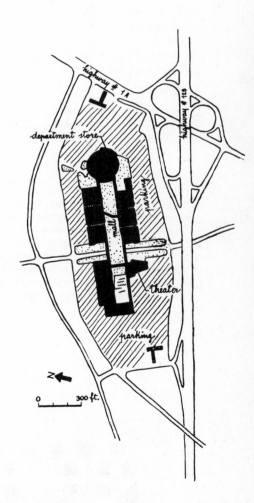

Right:
Turning its back to the highways by which its customers will arrive, this proposed center at Beverly, Mass., in the Boston suburban belt, is encircled by parking space (for 3000 cars), with the store fronts facing on an interior pedestrian mall. At the clover-leaf intersection of Highways 1A and 128, the center would be within 15 minutes driving distance of almost any point in the densely populated Boston suburban area, reaching out as far as Gloucester, Ipswich, Marblehead and Wakefield

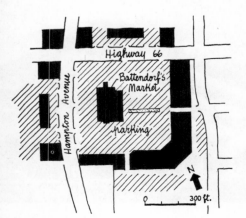

Left:
Enclosing the intersection of Hampton Boulevard and Highway 66 within its store-lined courtyard, Hampton Village shopping center is the result of 20 years work in site assembly and development by realtor Harry Brinkop. In the growing suburban area southwest of St. Louis, Mo., it is only 6 minutes drive, or less, from five other major highways. There is parking space for 2500 cars. The convenience and pulling power of the center already has been demonstrated by Bettendorf's Hampton Village Market, housed in the central island building. Last year this supermarket grossed more than $3½ million. Architect: Preston J. Bradshaw

195

Ben Kocivar Photo

Rehabilitation of an existing town center, though common in the bulky reports of planning experts, is usually forced into existence only at the impellent urge of some emergency or disaster. In Mount Kisco, N. Y., it was the need of eliminating two grade crossings which caused the New York Central Railroad to move their tracks (and the railroad station) about 200 ft. northwest. This in turn meant the demolition of many of the town's principal store buildings. Several of the merchants about to be displaced picked upon the area southeast of the present station as most desirable for expansion of the business center; and a series of three-way conferences between the staff of the Northern Westchester Joint Planning Program,

NORTH

relative distance from competing stores, will probably be far more important; more important even than the attractive appearance of the stores themselves as seen from the highway.

ZONING

A new shopping center must be fitted into the community zoning pattern. The traditional pattern of shallow business zones which run the length of major highways is being abandoned by forward-looking zoning ordinances. Such zoning encourage ribbon development (now generally frowned upon), and gives insufficient depth for off-street parking. Moreover it has been found that too large an area has usually been allotted to the business zone, when compared with an estimate of the number of stores which the surrounding community could be expected to need and be capable of supporting.

The tendency, therefore, in amending zoning controls is to confine the business areas to a limited number of strategic spots, with special regulation of off-street parking, advertising signs, etc. The aim always should be to make zoning controls flexible enough to allow

Designed for gradual expansion, this grouping of stores and community buildings for the town of West Covina, Calif., envisages a possible growth of population in the next 50 years from 2500 to a maximum of 55,000. It is hoped that it may be possible, through zoning regulations agreed upon by the property owners, to guide shopping center development into the plan shown here, with alternating pedestrian malls and vehicular service roads, and large parking areas between the store blocks. At present the area shown is still farmland. Architect: Robert E. Alexander

High land values in downtown shopping districts will often make multi-deck parking garages economically justifiable. The open-sided decks here are connected by ramps within the building perimeter. This garage is across the street from the department store which it serves. Connection between store and garage is underground by passages for pedestrians and conveyor belts for freight and packages. Customers returning to their car can pick up all their purchases at one time. Foley's, Houston, Tex. Architect: Kenneth Franzheim. Raymond Loewy Associates, Retail Planners & Designers

Paul Peters Photo

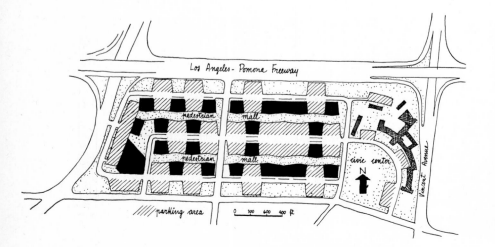

SHOPPING CENTERS

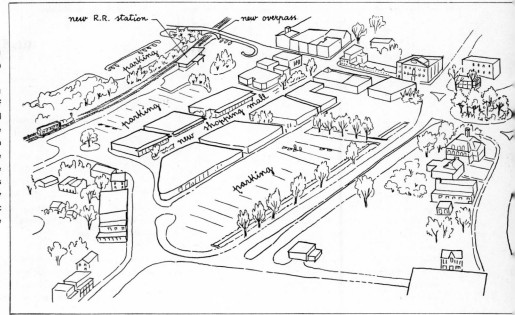

(Henry Fagin, director) the Mount Kisco Planning Board and the store owners, has brought forth the scheme of development pictured at right.

The main feature of the plan is a new shopping center on South Moger Ave. with the street itself converted into a landscaped pedestrian mall and extensive parking areas provided at the rear of the stores. Existing conditions are shown on the opposite page. A somewhat similar scheme was proposed some years ago to rehabilitate the shopping center of Rye, N. Y. Mount Kisco is depending upon agreement among the property owners concerned (fortunately few), with public support and realistic zoning rules, to guide future development according to the agreed plan

NORTH

for changing needs. However, the establishment of a new, major shopping center, with some 30 or 40 different stores and a theater, will almost always require extensive amendment of the local zoning ordinances.

TOPOGRAPHY

The shape and the size of the site always interpose themselves as modifying factors between the developer's program and the completed shopping center.

Is the site big enough to accommodate the number of stores (and the necessary amount of parking space for so many stores) upon which the developer's program is based? If not, is the land valuable enough to justify a multi-level plan, with roof parking, service tunnel, or the like?

Does the shape of the lot allow it to be developed economically? If it is not flat, can its contours be economically developed? How are the soil conditions, particularly for bearing and drainage?

Most of such questions can be answered only after quite extensive preliminary investigation, but it is never too late to abandon a site which cannot meet all foreseeable needs.

An irregular, sloping site will allow a two-level store with both levels directly accessible from a parking lot. The penthouse story is used for offices, storage, employees' dining room. This extended, rambling type of store (which suburban land values will justify) is typical of the country club atmosphere which New York's Lord & Taylor has so successfully expressed in its branch stores. This one is at Eastchester, N. Y., near the plushy, high-income, commuter suburbs section of Westchester County. Architects: Starrett & Van Vleck. Raymond Loewy Associates, Designers

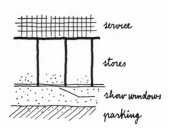
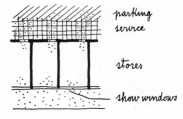
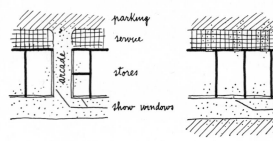

FRONT PARKING   REAR PARKING   REAR PARKING WITH ARCADES   SPLIT PARKING

PARKING AREAS & CIRCULATION

Front Parking

Customers at front, service at rear; completely separates the two circulations. The front show windows of the stores are set far back from the road and hidden behind parked cars.

Rear Parking

When customers are allowed to use the rear entrance there is necessarily some confusion between customer and service circulation. Many customers visiting a single store, entering and leaving at the rear, may never see the other store show windows.

Rear Parking with Arcades

The customer must make some detour in order to reach the store front entrance (rear entrances are supposedly reserved for service). By funneling this traffic, the arcades become very valuable display space. This sort of layout is most suitable for leisurely shopping (e.g., women's fashion goods) and is often used in combination with interior pedestrian malls.

Split Parking

The area in front of the stores is useful for quick in-and-out shopping (e.g., drug store, service stores), that at the rear for longer visits and overflow space. In this scheme the customers are sometimes allowed to use the rear store entrances, sometimes they are forced to detour through arcades between the stores to reach the front entrance.

SITE PLANNING

The most important influence on the site plan of shopping centers is circulation — of pedestrian shoppers, of their cars (parking), and of freight service for the stores.

The most practical solution, in our age of open planning and romantic merging of space, still remains the old-fashioned one of customers entrance and display windows on one side (the front), the service entrance and loading docks on the opposite side (the rear). An uneven site (usually rejected by store developers) may result in a special multi-level arrangement; but these are rare. Though the small stores in any center continue to have the traditional front and rear, the fronts may not face the highway. They may be turned around to face on a quiet interior court, landscaped and free of auto traffic. The service entrances will then front the highway.

As there is generally more space allotted to parking than to buildings, the parking area becomes the dominating feature of a shopping center site plan. It is an intermediate stage between the high-speed highway circulation and the pedestrian circulation within the stores. It may be placed in front of the stores — even though this front may not face the highway; this will be referred to here as *front parking*. Or it may be at the rear of the stores — even though such parking areas may adjoin the highway; this will be referred to as *rear parking*. The common compromise plan, with some front and some rear parking, will be known as *split parking*.

Front Parking is especially suitable for the fast "in-and-out" shopper. Many drugstore chains consider it almost as essential as a corner site.

It gives no flexibility between low and peak shopping hours. If it is planned to handle peak loads (according to the Urban Land Institute peak periods represent 15 to 20 per cent of the total number of store hours each week) it must be so large that the store fronts are set too far back from the street for normal convenience and display. The

Front parking extended by bending the line of stores and parking back into a deep and somewhat narrow courtyard at right angles to the main highway. For passing traffic a gas station is provided right on the highway, but otherwise the main road frontage is used for access rather than display. The rear (service) entrances of the stores which front the road at the left are hidden behind a high wall and a band of evergreen planting. The center is protected on three sides by residential development and a school. On the fourth side, across the highway, is golf course property. This Highland Park shopping center at Dallas, Tex., has proved so successful since Hugh Prather started it in 1931, that its plan (Fooshee & Cheek, architects) has been widely studied and followed, notably in the much publicized Bellevue Center, near Seattle, Wash. (opened in 1947)

Above:

Split parking is successfully used in this projected center on Route 4 near Hackensack, N. J. A restaurant and gas station are set directly on the highway; the other stores curve back to allow more frontage and sufficient front parking for normal business. The over-flow parking area behind is connected with the store fronts by several pedestrian arcades which pierce the store block. Notice that the island walkways in the parking lot are at right angles to the line of store fronts, so that they lead the shopper directly to the stores. Architects: Kelly & Gruzen

Below:

Rear parking (with a single line of front parking for the quick in-and-out shopper) is shown in this plan of the shopping center now building at Baldwin Hills Village, Los Angeles, Calif. The site is a strip 318 ft. deep between a main through highway (La Brea Avenue) and the residential area. The major stores are 125 ft. deep and have a rear entrance for customers from the parking lot. The minor stores, only 65 ft. deep, are sandwiched between, thus allowing for a series of screened service courts to serve both major and minor stores. The pedestrian way which bisects the center will later be extended by an overpass to connect with a projected additional shopping center on the other side of La Brea Avenue. Architect: Robert E. Alexander

passer-by on the highway is separated from the store fronts by a concealing mass of parked cars, or by a bleak expanse of empty pavement.

Split Parking overcomes these objections by providing a limited amount of front parking, an additional parking area for peak loads at rear or side.

Rear Parking must be divided into two categories, according to the route which the shopper takes in walking from parking space to stores and back again.

When shoppers enter through the rear of the store there is confusion between customer circulation and service circulation. The customer enters the store through a back door which is usually cluttered with supplies and empty crates. Window shopping is not encouraged, for many of the customers may never see the store front display, as they walk directly in and out of the rear entrance of a single store. Two exits complicate the layout and supervision of any store, especially self-service stores with check-out stations.

To overcome such objections a second category of rear parking plans keeps the rear entrances reserved for service; customers must walk through arcades cut between the stores and thus reach the front entrance. Such intensive funneling of traffic through these arcades makes them very valuable for the display and sale of impulse goods. Customers, however, tend to resent the detours to which they are subjected, and there is usually much undercover use of rear service entrances for greater convenience in going to and from parked cars.

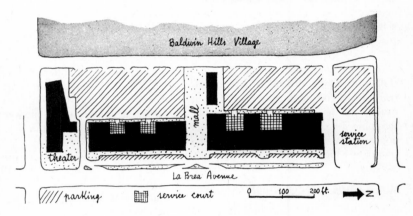

Below:

The rear entrance. Who's it for? Customers? Or freight and garbage? In most centers it is supposed to serve both purposes. Result: it serves neither as well as it could.

This is the customer. She can keep a store in business or put it into the bankruptcy court. Isn't it worth a little thought to avoid such shabby inconveniences?

Above:
Ground floor parking, with the whole building raised on stilts, enables the customer to go to and from her car under cover. Escalators could give quick and easy access to the stores above, and gravity chutes could be used to bring packages from the stores to pick-up points. Architects: Ketchum, Giná & Sharp

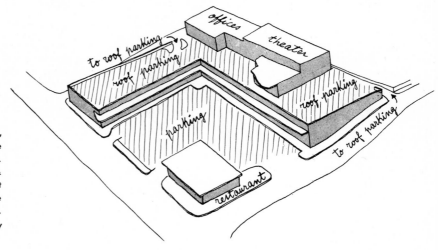

On a sloping site roof parking may become economically justified, particularly when it is possible to find a corner plot or a whole block with public street connection of upper and lower levels. The result in a case such as this (based on a design by Berla & Abel, architects, for College Park Shopping Center, Inc.) is that very little of the valuable site is wasted on ramps. On a flat site the ramps will be much longer and more wasteful of space (cf. page 212). In most cases, as here, the roof is supplemented by ground parking areas

Rear parking with arcades is especially suitable in site plans with a central landscaped mall. Such centers will usually be designed for more leisurely shopping (e.g., for fashion goods), as opposed to the quick, convenience shopping which is best served by front parking.

MULTI-LEVEL CIRCULATION

To overcome the rigid limitations of front (for customers and display) and rear (for service), customers and service may circulate on different levels. This may be of great help to the conscientious designer, but the decision must always be based finally on the answer to that standard question: Is it worth what it costs?

A service tunnel will segregate service and freight traffic, leaving all above ground free for customer circulation and private automobile parking. A tunnel is usually ruled out by its considerable extra cost, but may be justifiable where it is important to keep both front and rear of a store free for customers (see page 209).

Roof parking has always had a strong appeal to the modern designer for its three-dimensional circulation, and for its "functionalism" in putting to use an area which might otherwise appear wasted. Actually the economic facts of roof parking, and its effects upon circulation, have limited its use to a few special cases.

The necessary ramps leading from street level to roof are expensive to build

PARKING

These diagrams are based (with permission of the American Automobile Association) on the AAA *Parking Manual,* but with dimensions slightly increased to satisfy the special conditions found in shopping centers. A stall size of 20 ft. x 9 ft. has been chosen as roomy enough for boarding the car with large bundles.

292 sq. ft. per car **149 cars per acre**	**350 sq. ft. per car** **124 cars per acre**	**322 sq. ft. per car** **135 cars per acre**
90 degree parking is the least wasteful of space. It is recommended where land is expensive and the rate of turnover does not justify angle parking. It is used in almost all attendant garages. The large aisle required for the 90 degree turn permits two-way circulation	*45 degree parking* is not as economical in its use of space as the 90 degree pattern; but it is much easier to get in and out of the stalls	*60 degree parking* saves about 10 sq. ft. per car over the 45 degree arrangement, but needs more overall width because of the wider aisle. It is often used on plots too narrow for 90 degree parking, or where turnover is high and convenience in entering and leaving is important

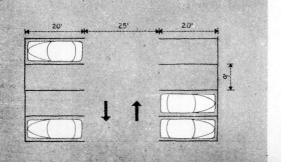

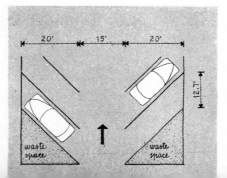

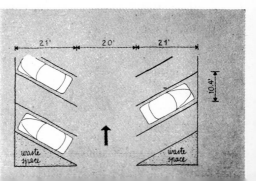

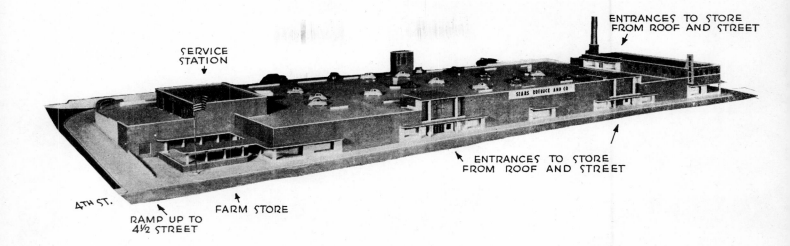

SERVICE STATION

ENTRANCES TO STORE FROM ROOF AND STREET

SEARS ROEBUCK AND CO

ENTRANCES TO STORE FROM ROOF AND STREET

4TH ST.

RAMP UP TO 4½ STREET

FARM STORE

Above:

Roof parking alone serves this Sears Roebuck store in Winston-Salem, N. C. The building itself fills the whole block depth between Fourth Street (in foreground) and Fourth & One Half Street. The latter is at roof level. The two streets are connected by a public road at one end, a ramp up the side of the building at the other. Shoppers' entrances to the store from street level and from the roof parking area are paired in a series of three stair towers. Architects: Shutze & Armistead

and waste valuable space which might be put to more productive use. A sloping site, which makes such ramps unnecessary, may provide economic justification for some roof parking, but supplementary ground parking usually will be essential.

The vertical circulation encouraged by roof parking is of greater advantage to a single large store (particularly a department store) than to a shopping center which consists mainly of smaller stores. The latter depends upon its

CIRCULATION
OF MOTORISTS ON FOOT

Right:

Most natural pattern for an easy flow of shoppers from cars to stores and back again is to have the parking lot aisles at right angles to the store fronts. Pedestrians can use the roadway or walkstrips set between the rows of parked cars. To be of any use such walkstrips must be wide enough to allow for bumper overhang on each side and still leave space for two people carrying bundles to walk abreast.

For shallow curb parking, aisles parallel to the store fronts are far more economical of space. This is equally true, of course, when this type of shallow front parking is carried into a deep court off the road (see page 198). It does make it more difficult for the shoppers to go from car to store and back again, worming between cars, if they cannot find space in the single row alongside the curb

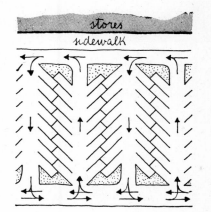

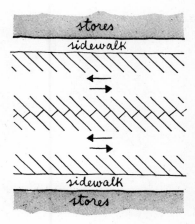

310 sq. ft. per car   140 cars per acre

Herringbone parking—here shown at 45 degrees without reducing size of stalls or aisles, saves the wasted triangle of space at the front of each parked car which occurs in all other angle parking layouts

Parallel line flow where all cars are parked in the same direction (left). The driver entering a fully occupied aisle must make a wide detour around the whole parking area before coming back to the same end to try the next row. (see page 203, for controlled version)

Back and forth flow, with one-way traffic, up one aisle and down the next (below). This makes the finding of an empty stall a much less lengthy business, for the driver goes up one aisle and, if he finds no empty space, simply turns around the end and goes down the neighboring aisle

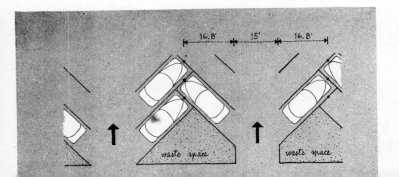

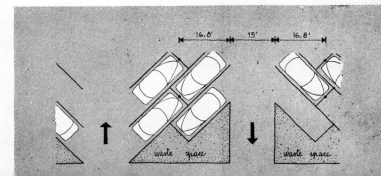

Sears Roebuck & Co. have been among the outstanding pioneers in the provision of off-street parking for their retail store customers. They have tried roof parking (see page 201) and ground parking and various combinations of the two. Here, in their new store at Houston, Texas, they have given a new and convincing efficiency to the management of ground parking by making sure that the large parking space is used to its utmost capacity

A controller, from the windows of a room high up in one corner of the tower, overlooks the whole area. The parking aisles are all one-way with 60 degree stalls. At the store end of each aisle, along the service road by which all cars enter the lot, is a traffic light managed by the controller in the tower. In normal operation, as long as there is a single empty stall in an aisle the traffic light at its end will show a green arrow. When the aisle is full the con-

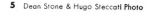

Motorists as pedestrians. There is some dangerous confusion when pedestrians and motorists share the same aisles in the parking lot, particularly if there is two-way traffic (2). Raised walkway strips between the cars (1), if they are to be used, must lead in the right direction, toward the store front and not parallel to it, and be sufficiently wide to leave walking space for two abreast in spite of bumper overhang. This means at least 7 ft. wide, and better 10 ft. Where the parking aisles run parallel to the store front there may be a clearly marked passage for pedestrians, through the lines of cars and across the open aisles (3).

The Missing Link is between the cash-and-carry supermarket and the automobile which the shopper is using as delivery van. The supermarket may provide attentive, white-aproned squires to carry the heavy, bulky packages (4). Or some type of wheeled carts. Both are unproductive expenses as far as the merchant is concerned. For weather-protected loading he may provide a porte-

cochere, a step away from the main entrance—to avoid congestion—but connected to it by a covered walk (5). Designed by Raymond Loewy Associates. Better still he could set up an underground moving belt to carry the packages to a pick-up station in the parking lot (6). This should give a considerable saving in personnel and, with space allowed for a sufficient "magazine" of waiting cars, should cause no congestion within the parking area. From a project by Raymond Loewy Associates.

The other possibility is "auto-shopping." Based on the same principle as the filling station and the increasingly popular auto-bank, "auto-shopping" aisles (7) permit quick purchases of standard goods and errands at laundry and dry cleaner without leaving the car. Auto-shopping does not eliminate, but simply complements selective shopping done on foot; conventional shops can be seen at the upper level, connected to the parking area by an overpass. Howard T. Fisher & Associates, Inc., Architects and Engineers

3

4

5

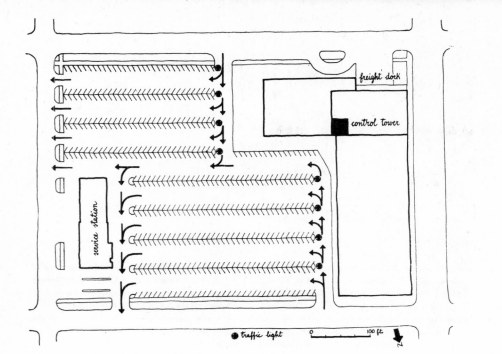

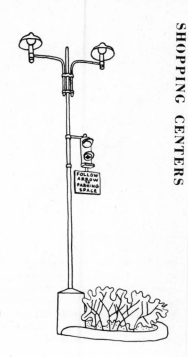

troller will immediately switch that light to red. Some control system of this type is particularly necessary when the aisles are as long as they are here, making it extremely difficult for the arriving motorist to see from one end if there are any empty stalls.

A further economy in the use of a limited parking space is to empty the one-way aisles directly on to a side road, instead of providing a service road within the site. Such an arrangement would scarcely be possible without the tower controller.

It is interesting to notice that the freight loading dock, which one would normally expect to find at the rear of the building has been moved to a recess on the street front, where it does not interfere with the customer entrance from the parking lot. Architect: Kenneth Franzheim.

largest store — the supermarket or department store — to entice the traffic, the window-shopping pedestrians, upon which the smaller stores depend for a livelihood (and for which they are paying high rent). If the big store has roof parking, shoppers may not see and visit the smaller surrounding stores at all.

One advantage of roof parking which is often overlooked is the way in which it discourages the pirate parker who uses the shopping center parking space but trades with the competing stores across the street where no parking space is provided. The deterrent here is probably inconvenience rather than shame.

Under-store parking, a favorite of Le Corbusier and many another grand-scale planner, would have the advantage of protecting the shopper from the weather all the way from car to market and back again. Escalators would carry the shoppers up to the stores above. Unlike roof parking no space is wasted on ramps. Some merchants would deplore the lack of ground-level, street-front display space in such a scheme.

Multi-deck parking garages may be economically justified on expensive downtown sites. They are usually considered unsuitable for self-parking, though J. C. Nichols in his Country Club Shopping District in Kansas City, has had a three-level one in successful operation for several years. But for self-parking, ramps must be made wider and less steep.

The final compelling fact, though, will probably remain the answer to the old question: Is it worth the cost?

PARKING AREA SIZE

How much parking space should be provided? Here is the most important, most widely disputed, and most incon-

6

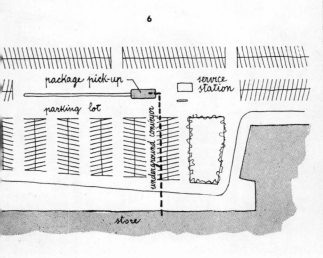

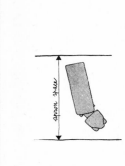
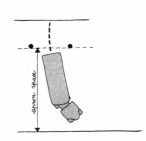
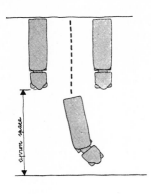
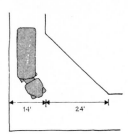

14' 24'

The diagrams show the amount of space which should be allowed for maneuvering tractor-trailers in and out of a loading dock. The amount of apron space will depend on the over-all length of the tractor-trailer, and the width of the opening into which it must back. This is shown in the table at right. The apron spaces given are minimum for

backing into a dock in one maneuver. The most common height for loading docks is 44 to 50 ins., though light trucks have a lower bed level. Overhead clearance should be 14 ft., for standard trailers range up to 12 ft. 6 ins. in height. Special loads, such as heavy machinery, may need greater clearance. Maximum width of the standard trans-

port units is 8 ft., so that a minimum clearance of 10 ft. should be allowed. If there is a right angle turn in a narrow driveway extra space must be allowed on the inside of the turn (as illustrated in the sketch directly above) for the cut-in of the trailer wheels. (All figures supplied by Fruehauf Trailer Co.)

SHOPPING CENTERS

clusively answered question of them all.

The safest guides are presumably past experience combined with knowledge of local conditions (type of stores, local shopping habits, available public transportation). Indications are, however, that the more parking space provided, the more people decide to shop by car, and so the more parking space is needed.

The Urban Land Institute recommends a 2:1 ratio between parking area and floor area of stores. This is for "average conditions." In centers which rely almost exclusively on automobile shoppers (particularly in the West) a

ratio of 3:1 is now becoming common.

An important consideration here is the type of shopping which is expected at the center, whether leisurely selection such as we expect with women's fashions, or quick in-and-out transactions at drug stores, banks, service shops.

J. C. Nichols, in his Country Club Plaza, at Kansas City, counts on a turnover of 5 to 8 cars per day in each parking space. The designers of the North Shore Center, near Boston, are assuming a daily turnover of 3.5.

Waverly Taylor, a shopping center developer in Washington, D. C., came to the conclusion that a ratio of 2:1 was

a necessary minimum, even where 60 per cent of the customers arrived on foot.

A more complex method of calculating the parking area required is to base it upon the expected annual gross sales of the stores. Assuming an average daily sales volume, an average dollar volume per sale, an average number of sales per customer, an average number of customers per car, an average daily turnover in the parking area, it is possible to find the number of parking stalls required in an average day. Multiplied by an assumed peak factor, this will give the number of stalls required to

Transfer of freight from truck to store shelves has too often been as makeshift as the customer's transfer of bulky packages from store to automobile. Gradually some more efficient systems are emerging. The use of sectional gravity roller conveyors is increasing, not only for transferring the goods from truck to store but also for moving goods within the store. By combining this with a motor-operated conveyor belt between floors, as shown below, the basement becomes accessible storage area. (First National Stores.)

Another system (illustrated below) designed to cut handling costs uses large standard bins holding about 60 cases of merchandise. Ten of these bins form a truck load. They are loaded and unloaded with a fork lift truck, then wheeled about the store on hydraulic lifts. (Designed by Raymond Loewy Associates, for Lucky Market.) This, like many other busy supermarkets, depends upon night work by stock clerks to have the shelves filled, ready for next morning's customers

Dean Stone — Hugo Steccati Photo

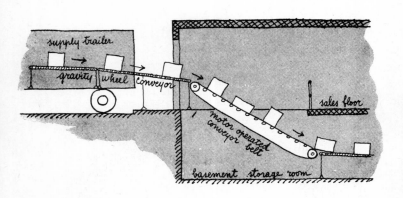

"Apron" Space Required by Tractor-Trailer for
One Maneuver into or out of Position (Measured
from Outermost Vehicle or Other Obstruction)

Over-all Length of Tractor-Trailer	Width of Opening	Apron Space Required
35'	10'	46'
	12'	43'
	14'	39'
40'	10'	48'
	12'	44'
	14'	42'
45'	10'	57'
	12'	49'
	14'	48'

Right:

Flexibility in store widths can be neatly obtained even with a uniform span (here it is 14 ft.). The lally columns with stone casing form solid dividing posts; the one left bare in the two-bay store is quite inconspicuous behind the center entrance. Ridgeway Shopping Center, Stamford, Conn. Designer: Alfons Bach

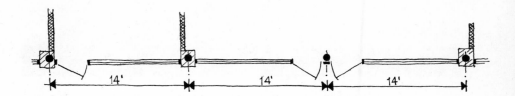

satisfy demand "on the last shopping day before Christmas." The beginner might well be frightened by this volume of assumptions and run back to depend on other operators' experience.

STORE BUILDINGS

Even more than most building types, the shopping center is still in the stage of groping and experiment. As experience grows, preferences change. The few generalizations gathered here reflect the opinions of many developers old and new. Such experience must, of course, be tempered by the local conditions of each job.

Right:

People and fixtures are the units which determine the most usable store widths. A typical section of average people and average fixtures will give a minimum usable width of about 12 ft. or 14 ft. with a display case at the side of the aisle. Of course, double racks for garment storage will be 3 ft. 6 in. wide, rather than the 2 ft. common in most other storage fixtures; but then there won't be need for a counter case. Naturally, all these dimensions (except the customer aisle width) mean nothing if the store is divided into two sections crossways by a counter parallel to the store front. This latter arrangement is often found in service stores

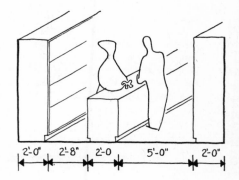

Below:

A variety of store depths is commonly achieved by projecting each store building as far as the tenant requires into an irregular service court with employee parking. To increase the size of any store it may either be extended further into the rear court or take over some space from one or both of its neighbors. There is only a single entrance from the street to this rear service court, so that it is effectively shielded from the view of shoppers. This sort of arrangement, a favorite of that vastly experienced Kansas City realtor, J. C. Nichols, is particularly suitable for downtown sites with a single row of front parking

A staggered line of stores gives each store a rear dock at which a truck can load or unload without blocking the one-way service road. It also allows for a wide and useful variety in store depths, ranging from 84 ft. down to 48 ft. A separate parking area for tenants ensures that their all-day parking will not sterilize any part of the customers' front parking space. Aero Acres, wartime development for Glenn L. Martin Co., at Middle River, Md. Consulting architects: Skidmore, Owings & Merrill

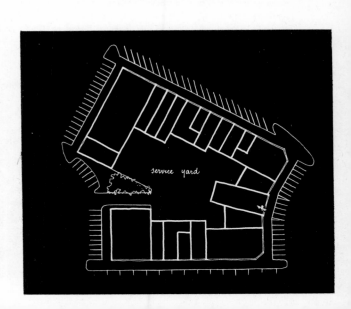

Gottscho-Schleisner Photo

Depth of store buildings varies widely, with a tendency by supermarkets to demand 150 ft. where before they were used to 100 ft. or 125 ft. Local fire regulations which demand more exits once a store exceeds some given depth, and strip zoning for business which holds the stores in a narrow bank alongside the highway, are often controlling factors when a decision has to be made. To provide the greatest possible flexibility, so that changes of tenancy with different space demands may be economically satisfied, is the developer's overriding ambition. A common expedient is to provide space for expansion at the rear (often combined with rear parking), so that each store can be of different depth. Keeping the rear wall a curtain wall free of ducts, pipes, etc., will permit it to be demolished easily and re-erected in a different position.

Basement stairs (above) need to be wide, shallow, inviting, if they are to seem worth climbing. Customers are always more willing to walk downstairs than to walk up, and for this reason basement space is often considered more valuable to a store than second floor space. This lower level at Lord & Taylor's suburban branch store at Eastchester, N. Y., opens out on one side at ground level to a parking area (see page 197). Architects: Starrett & Van Vleck. Raymond Loewy Associates, Designers

By a juggling of levels (below) what would otherwise be a basement becomes an attractive ground floor space fronting on a landscaped pedestrian mall; and the space above, which might seem an inaccessible second story, is practically at ground level as the shopper approaches from the parking area. The result is two equally attractive and accessible floors of selling space. To make the difference in level appear even less important, communication between the two floors is by ramps instead of stairs.

The other favorite expedient, which is particularly applicable to certain difficult-shape lots, is to fit smaller stores into the angles when the main line of store fronts turns a corner.

Width of store buildings. Here flexibility is, if anything, more important than in the case of store depth. The ideal shopping center would be a continuous roof and floor with a clear open space between them uncluttered with any supporting pillars. All partition walls could be taken down and put up again — without any new material — within a few hours. While they are waiting for this to become structurally possible, designers do the best they can by

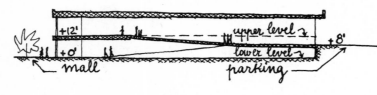

Canopies are gradually becoming one of the shopping center's standard amenities, a typical necessity in a one-story building group with outside circulation. This permanent canopy (1) sensibly includes built-in-sidewalk lighting. (Ridgeway, Stamford, Conn.; Alfons Bach Associates, Designers.) The light impermanence of brightly colored canvas on a pipe frame (2) gives a garden party mood to this suburban department store catering to women with a sense of fashion. (Lord & Taylor, Manhasset, N. Y.; Starrett & Van Vleck, Architects, Raymond Loewy Associates, Designers.) With calculated precision these blades (3) combine sun shading and ventilation, in a region where sun is more impelling than rain. (Bullocks, Pasadena, Calif.; Wurdeman & Becket, Architects.)

Signs within a shopping center may often be confined to certain uniform positions; to catch the attention of passing motorists signs must be high—this one (4) is 65 ft.— and set at right angles to the traffic flow. A row of large, brightly-lighted windows is further bait. (Lucky Market, San Leandro, Calif.; Raymond Loewy Associates, Designers.) Such restriction as this (5), with uniform signs, uniform lettering, can rarely be imposed by anybody less powerful than a U. S. government agency. (Linda Vista, Calif.; National Housing Administration.) But signs may be confined, e.g., within a band of corrugated transite (6), lit by a battery of torpedo lights, which throw light also on the sidewalk. (Oakland Gardens, Long Island, N. Y.; B. Braunstein, Architect)

E. M. Demerest Photo   **1**   Ben Greenhaus Photo   **2**   Julius Shulman Photo   **3**

keeping spans as wide as economically justified. Span widths must also be related to common store widths, which are based in turn upon more or less standard fixture dimensions. A side wall cabinet, plus a serving aisle, plus a counter cabinet, plus a customer aisle, gives a total store width of about 12 ft. This is consequently a common unit width. However, more and more stores are now favoring less conventional layouts. These fall outside the computations based on what was formerly standard fixture layout — another argument for extreme flexibility.

In any case it would usually be reasonable to have fixed equipment such as plumbing stacks and heating mains repeat every 24 ft., so that they will be available to serve a series of 12 ft. units. Further variation in width can be gained by some offsetting of partitions, without losing advantage of the original modular layout.

Ceiling height is always related to width and depth, the bigger the higher. Modern lighting and air conditioning make ceilings of more than 12 ft. unnecessary in even the largest store unit. In small shops 9 ft. should be sufficient. Of course these heights do not include the space which must be allowed for ductwork above the finished ceiling.

With a mezzanine floor, a minimum ceiling height of 16 ft. is necessary. To provide equivalent space in a basement is usually much cheaper. When basements are to be used by customers, whether as part of the store's selling area, or merely for services such as toilet rooms, the clear ceiling height should not be less than 9 ft. after allowance for air conditioning ducts, which here become essential equipment.

Basements and upper stories. Are they worth their cost? In the case of basements, an almost unanimous yes. The cost of basement space is normally low, especially in those parts of the country where footings have to be carried three or four feet below grade. If basement space is to be used for selling, it can be made much more inviting (and so more profitable) by a wide stair well in a prominent position with a flight of wide, shallow stairs.

Second story offices for doctors, dentists and professional men are found in many centers, but there seems to be some doubt about whether they really pay their keep. However, they certainly make the public think of the shopping center as a place where one goes for *everything*, and they may well bring some new customers to the stores. On an uneven site there are considerable possibilities for making a direct entrance from the road to the second story, which immediately increases its possible usefulness. Even on a comparatively flat site it may pay to adjust the levels so that each of the two floors opens on ground level at one side.

Equipment. The practice in most centers is to give each tenant his own heating (and often cooling) plant, on which he pays fuel and maintenance costs. Most shopping center owners claim that shopkeepers would be wasteful of heat were it to be supplied from a single plant serving the whole group of stores.

However, to make sure that the tenants are not stingy in the use of their equipment (particularly their cooling), in some leases it is specified that this equipment *must* be put into operation once the temperature reaches a certain level.

In the same way the tenants are usually compelled to keep their show windows lit till a specified hour in the evening, and to stay open late one or two nights a week.

8

7

Flowers and children mean trouble and expense for the shopping center promoter; but attention to their needs will pay highly in goodwill. A children's playground or nursery is one of the most popular amenities which a shopping center can provide, particularly in a neighborhood center where most of the customers walk to the stores (8). Nurseries are often proposed, few actually exist. (Levittown, Long Island, N. Y.; Alfred J. Levitt & Sons, developers.) Benches beneath a spreading oak (7) offer rest and shade to tired mothers and fretful children. (Fresh Meadows, Long Island, N. Y.; Voorhees, Walker, Foley & Smith, Architects)

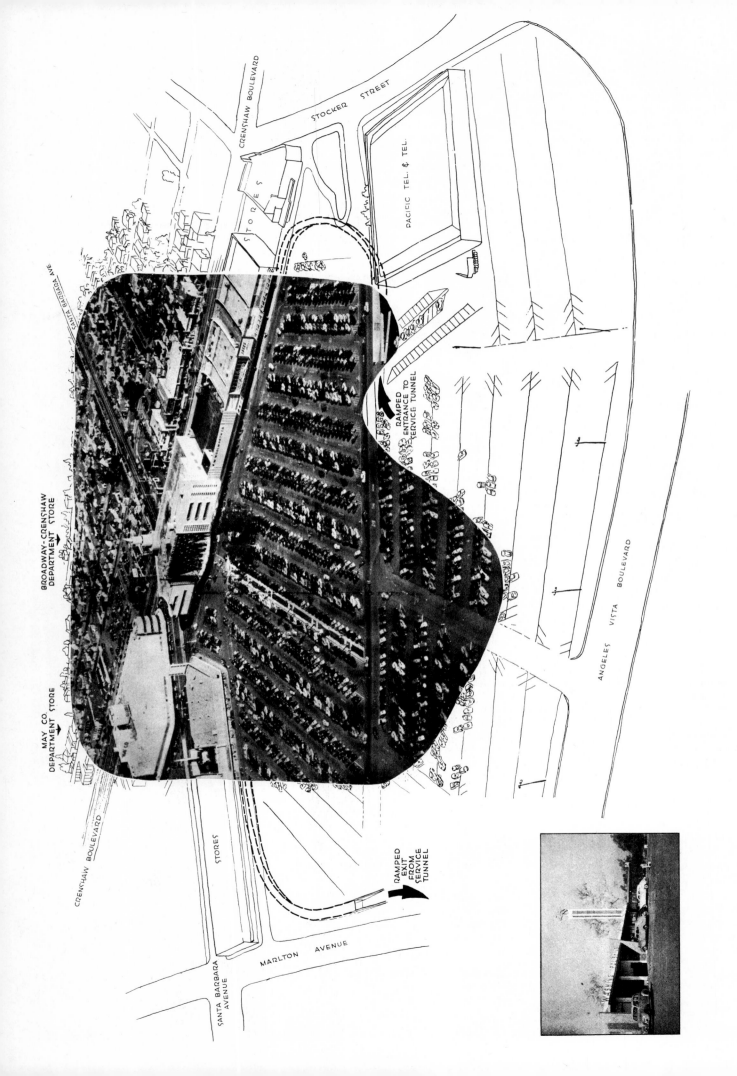

STOCKER STREET

CRENSHAW BOULEVARD

PACIFIC TEL. & TEL.

STORES

SANTA BARBARA AVE.

BROADWAY-CRENSHAW
DEPARTMENT STORE

MAY CO.
DEPARTMENT STORE

RAMPED
ENTRANCE TO
SERVICE TUNNEL

ANGELES VISTA BOULEVARD

CRENSHAW BOULEVARD

STORES

RAMPED
EXIT
FROM
SERVICE
TUNNEL

SANTA BARBARA
AVENUE

MARLTON AVENUE

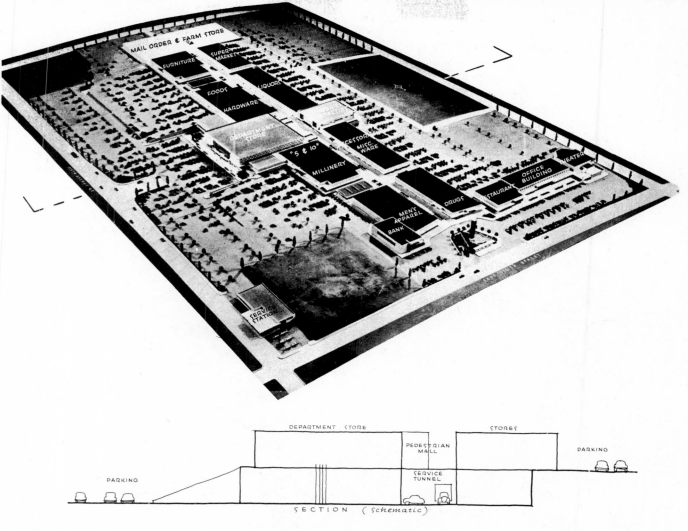

 Kenneth S. Brown Photo

A change of level gives the Bon Marché two "ground floors," accessible at ground level on the mall side, the other on the parking side.

SERVICE TRAFFIC CONFINED TO UNDERGROUND TUNNELS

LEFT

THE BROADWAY department store, developers of Broadway-Genshaw shopping center in Los Angeles, realized that the majority of their customers would be arriving by automobile and approach the stores from the 10-acre parking lot in the rear. They also expected pedestrians to enter from the street front, a fast-growing shopping avenue. Each store therefore has two fronts, one on the street, the other on the parking lot. All service traffic is relegated to a tunnel, 20 ft. wide and almost ½ mile long, with loading docks in the basement. The added cost was justified by the improved appearance and display value of the rear front, which becomes, like the street front, a windowshopper's walk sheltered by a wide overhang. Stores are 150 ft. deep. The four-story Broadway department store façade is clear of openings above the street level and

serves as a billboard for displays seen from the parking area. Architect: Albert B. Gardiner.

ABOVE

NIPPED between Puget Sound and Lake Washington, Seattle can expand with ease only north or south (see map); though the Floating Bridge has speeded development of the eastern side of the lake (Bellevue's new shopping center capitalizes on this population movement). The projected Northgate shopping center will serve a population of about 300,000, increasing at an annual rate of about 9000. The 66-acre site is between major highways (see arrow on map).

The plan has a long pedestrian mall with a service tunnel beneath. Arcades between stores join this mall and the parking areas. The food stores and hard lines are at one end, the volume traffic-

getter (Bon Marché department stores) right in the center, and at the other end the apparel and soft lines. For protection and possible expansion, the promoters have bought most of the adjoining land. Architects: John Graham & Co.

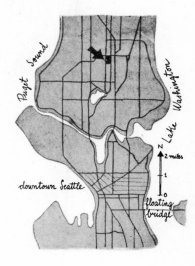

← The pylon sign of this gas station shows up clearly from every one of the 2000 parking stalls. Architect: Albert B. Gardner, Associates: Wolfe & Thormin.

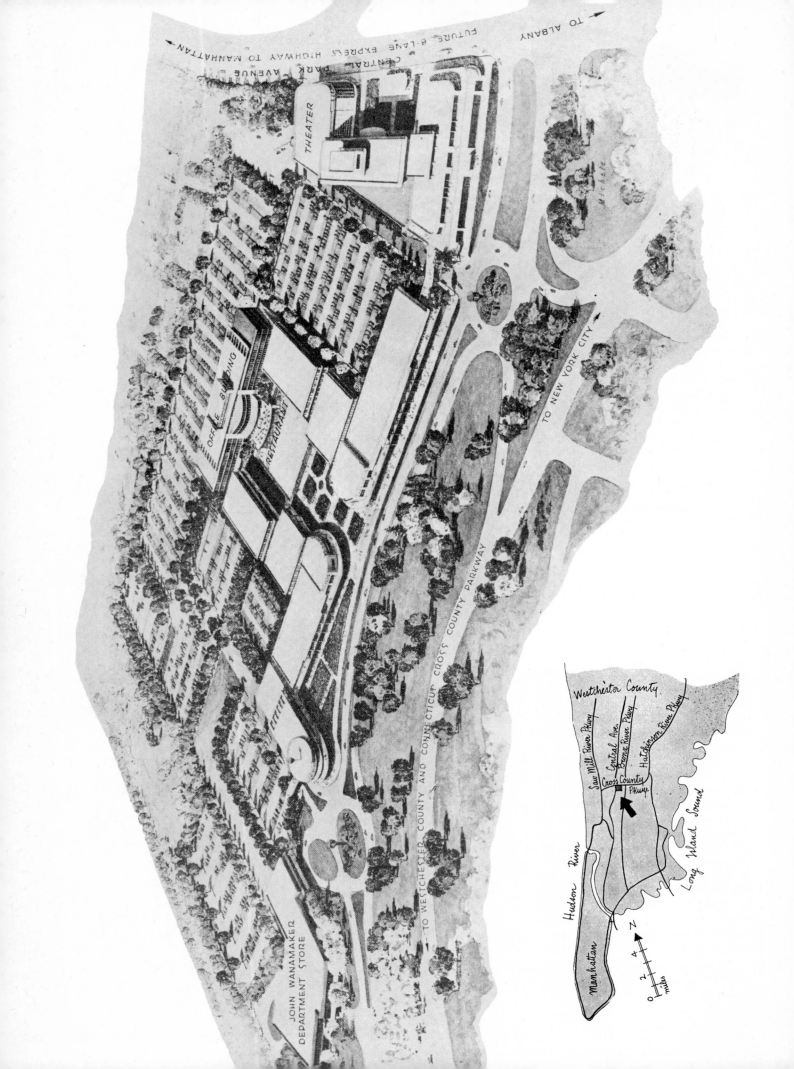

← WHERE THE CITY MEETS THE SUBURBS

Harris & Brown, Architects

ON the narrow neck of land where Manhattan and the Bronx start to spread out into the Westchester County and Connecticut suburbs is the proposed Cross County shopping center. At Yonkers, N. Y., it is enmeshed in a net of parkways and expressways at the intersection of the Cross County Parkway and Central Avenue (an extension of the Bronx's busy Grand Concourse). Within a short bus ride are the densely populated areas of the Bronx and Yonkers. Within easy driving distance by parkway are most of the rich New York suburbs. The 60-acre site has been specially rezoned for business use. The new center will cater to the neighborhood trade with supermarkets, service stores, and a movie theater, to the passing motorist with restaurants and filling stations, and to the regional trade with branch department and chain fashion stores. The added possibilities of its position near Manhattan are reflected in the proposal for a five-story office building at one end.

The central pedestrian mall has been carefully proportioned to combine the most spacious appearance with the shortest possible distance between one store block and another. The department store (John Wanamaker) is set in an unusual position on slightly rising ground at one edge of the center. It is hoped that it will draw traffic from Central Avenue (on to which the parkway clover-leaf also debouches) through the rest of the development.

TRIANGULAR SITE SUGGESTS CIRCULAR MALL

Kelly & Gruzen, Architects

THE MAYBROOK shopping center, now building at Maywood, N. J., is set on a triangular site at the junction of two main highways.

The plan of the center has been most ingeniously accommodated within this triangle. The theater is set somewhat apart from the stores at the apex of the triangle. In the wide base of the triangle is the circle of stores surrounding a landscaped pedestrian mall dotted with smaller booths. Arcades between the store blocks lead from this mall to the parking area.

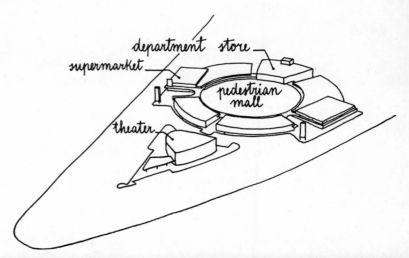

Louis Checkman Photo

William Eccles Photo

ROOF PARKING MODIFIES STORE LAYOUT

Gruen & Krummeck, Architects

IN the center of residential Westchester, in the suburban area southwest of Los Angeles, Calif., Frank H. Ayres & Sons have laid out a 72-acre shopping center with parking space for some 3500 cars.

Stores are set along the highways in a strip 500 ft. deep. With a store block 150 ft. in depth, the remaining 350 ft. should give sufficient parking area. But Milliron's department store required

a building twice the standard depth which would leave insufficient space for parking. So for this store the ground parking area has been supplemented with roof parking. This in turn fitted in with two other new ideas: a main entrance from the roof via escalator to the center of the store, with the various departments opening out in different colored quadrants from the center circle (all advertisements refer to these various "stores" by color); and the addition of a penthouse story containing a restaurant and auditorium, (also a beauty shop and a nursery in which customers may park their children) which, being independent of the rest of the store, may be kept open later evenings and Sundays.

The roof accommodates 220 cars. Each of the one-way ramps serving it is 20 ft. wide, so that no woman shopper should be frightened off by the unaccustomed conditions of a drive-up store. At present this parking area is supplemented not only by the ground

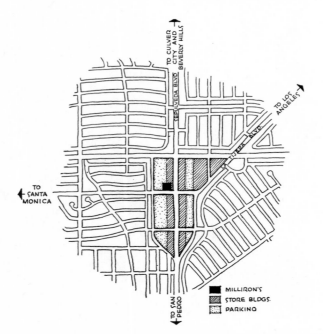

MILLIRON'S
STORE BLDGS.
PARKING

Julius Shulman Photos

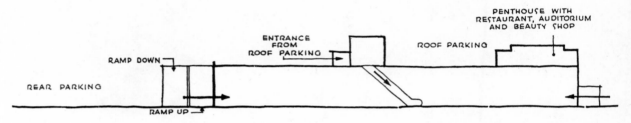

PENTHOUSE WITH
RESTAURANT, AUDITORIUM
AND BEAUTY SHOP

ENTRANCE
FROM
ROOF PARKING

ROOF PARKING

RAMP DOWN

REAR PARKING

RAMP UP

SECTION THROUGH CENTER OF STORE

space behind Milliron's, but also by that behind a proposed store block to the north. If and when those stores are built, it seems probable that the total parking space will be insufficient.

Shopper circulation, as estimated by the architects, shows the central entrance from the roof carrying as much or more traffic as the entrances from the rear parking area and from the street fronts. The symmetrical, radiating layout of fixtures is unusual in the modern department store, which tends to favor a series of free-form islands. The Center Circle, with the heaviest traffic, contains the merchandise normally found on the ground floor of a department store; the Rose store is for women's clothes, the Green store for men's and children's wear, the Blue store contains appliances and furniture, the Yellow store other household goods

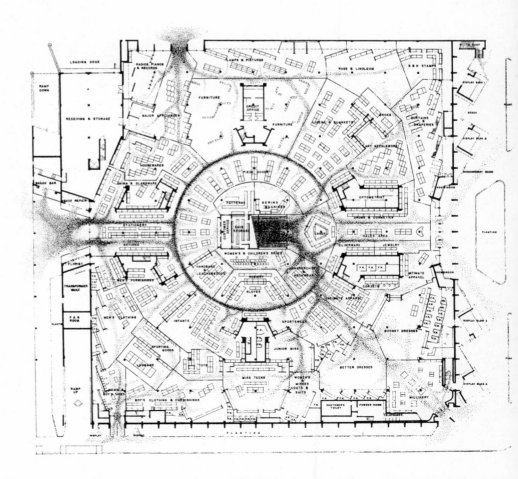

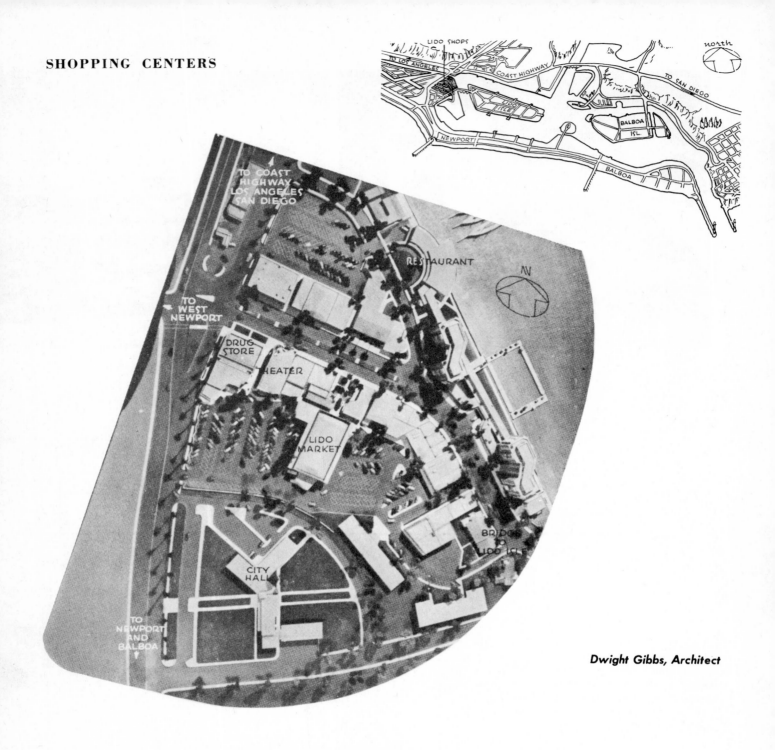

Dwight Gibbs, Architect

CUSTOMERS COME IN BOATS AS WELL AS AUTOS

BRANCHING off the Coast Highway to reach Balboa and Lido Isle (see map), motorists inevitably pass through the Griffith Co.'s Lido Shops development now under construction at Newport Beach, Calif. And then later, having got into their vacation clothes and gone aboard one of the 5000 pleasure craft in the harbor, they return by water to the Lido Shops anchorage, go ashore to the special Ship's Galley maintained by the Lido supermarket, and order supplies enough for a cruise.

As this whole seaside area is changing gradually from a summer resort to a year-round community, Lido Shops' position, straddling a highway bottleneck and across the street from a good anchorage, becomes increasingly important. So far built are a theater, drugstore and supermarket. A restaurant with terraces hanging out over the water is already under construction; plans are in hand for a hotel and apartment house to occupy the rest of the waterfront. The new city hall is on the inland side of the store group.

In line with local custom the stores are built without basements. To provide storage space, and to give an imposing two-story front, there is a mezzanine floor at the rear. This is used mainly for storage. The merchandise is lifted from the freight dock by a belt conveyor, then sent where needed in the store by gravity feed.

All exterior painting and landscaping conforms to a standardized color chart prepared by the architect; and all exterior signs must be approved by a committee of owner, architect and advertising counsel.

Left: the landscaped parking area at the rear of Lido Market. Below: the street front of Lido Market is set back behind palms and flowerbeds

Floyd Hopkins Photo

The two-story-high glass front of the drug-store makes an impressive showing on the main road corner next to the movie theater

Although most customers enter center from rear, street side was accorded more importance in recognition of public's window shopping habits. Covered walk, 10 ft wide, runs length of center and provides shop front protection which permits use of hard wood glass sets and natural woods as well as plastic surfaces on doors

MIRACLE CENTER SHOPPING DEVELOPMENT *North Hollywood, California*

Benedict, Hutchison, Kinsey
Walter G. Benedict, Architect

Kersey Kinsey Company, Builders

Julius Shulman

Pedestrian arcade connects boulevard front of center with community parking area at rear. Eggcrate canopy and palm trees shade store-lined arcade at front and rear. Stores on both sides of arcade extend half way to rear with display windows on arcade. Two offices open on arcade

THIS small shopping center at Coldwater Canyon, North Hollywood, developed before the area around it had been completely built up, now serves a community of some 2000 persons. Its organization of shops and customer facilities within a framework of simplicity is still an oasis of orderly design in the area.

To offset the inducements of an existing supermarket, Miracle Center had to create its own attractions, but with an eye to the budget. This it did by the careful use of landscaping: the parking lot behind the shops is extensively landscaped, and a walk from parking area to shops is lined with trees whose shade is welcome on the many very hot days of spring, summer and fall. A covered walk along the shop fronts is a further attraction to customers coming and going between supermarket and parking place.

Sign control by the owner, a stipulation of each lease, has been so far only about 60 per cent successful, and the clause has not been completely enforceable. The architects report that a program of tenant education is in progress.

The cost of the center, including architects' fees, landscaping, signs and parking area, came to $130,000 or $7 per sq ft (additional mechanical work for drug store is figured in this).

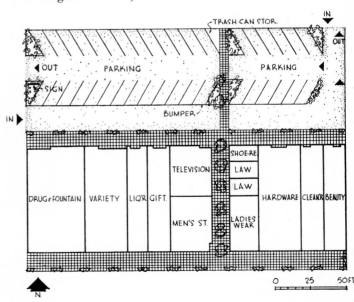

Gottscho-Schleisner

HOW ONE SPACE BECAME FOUR

Showroom and Offices for "Scarves by Vera," New York

Marcel Breuer, Architect

IN THIS DEFTLY HANDLED ALTERATION, a central problem was to provide a showroom for women's scarves where buyers from rival stores could be accommodated simultaneously with the proper degree of privacy. In addition, the program called for two private offices and a general office — all to be crammed into an area 37 by 42 and to be ready for business within two months!

A major design question was how to handle the bulky existing column poised slightly off center in the main space. This difficulty was transformed into an asset by girding the shaft with the showroom's most unusual and attractive feature: a display case unit that reaches out four fins to define four separate sales areas. This is accomplished without destroying the unity of the showroom volume. (Detail on page 222.) The four-part division is further augmented by treating each of the enclosing walls in a different fashion: one is draped in gray flannel, another painted electric blue, a third

covered by a photo mural, while the fourth is faced with sheet cork upon which ordinary bottle corks are cemented in a regular pattern which sets up an interesting decorative shadow rhythm. (Detail on page 221.)

Each sales station contains a table and chairs: the tables, architect-designed, consist of a black lacquered 1⅛-in. plywood top supported by a welded frame of ⅝-in. square steel bars painted gray; the chairs are the newest Eames design, leather covered.

The acoustical ceiling is suspended 3 ft below the existing one to bring it down to an 8 ft 6 in. height for good scale, and at the same time provide room for ducts and recessed lighting fixtures. The ceiling terminates

14 in. away from the walls, both for visual separation and to yield space for concealed peripheral lighting. The architect's conception for lighting, i.e., the strong texture light on all walls which spills enough into the room for a soft over-all effect, supplemented by downlights above the tables, has proved to be extremely successful. (Detail on page 221.)

In the office spaces, an economical and attractive new ceiling consists of an open framework of 2 by 6s painted white which contains standard fluorescent troffers arranged in a staggered pattern. Ducts, pipes and the old ceiling over are painted dark gray, creating the illusion of a void above. (Detail on page 221.)

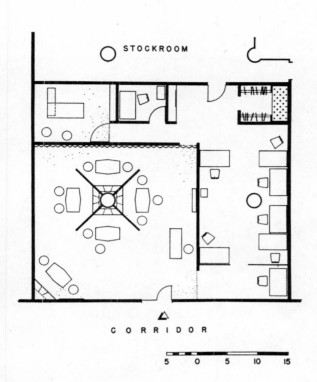

General view as one enters, left page, shows how four comparatively private sales stations have been created without sacrificing the spatial unity of the room. Entrance wall, next left, is cork covered—mirror on fixed door leaf adds depth and glitter. Rear wall, above, is draped with a medium gray wool flannel of the sort widely used for men's business suits

Gottscho-Schleisner

The photo-mural wall was designed by Herbert Matter, who determined that black and white would be most effective in relation to the other wall treatments. The view above reveals its scale and effect in the room; the montage at left shows the entire panel. The leaf is a favorite design motif of the owner-designer, Vera, and her leaf designs have been perennial best sellers

Drawing by Tom Ballenger

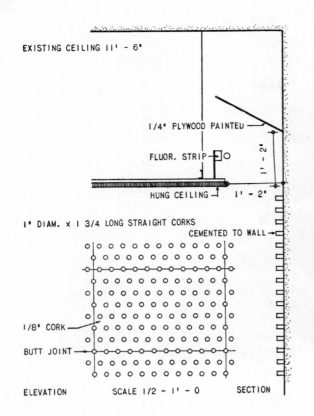

EXISTING CEILING 11' - 6"

1/4" PLYWOOD PAINTED

FLUOR. STRIP

1' - 2"

HUNG CEILING   1' - 2"

1" DIAM. × 1 3/4 LONG STRAIGHT CORKS

CEMENTED TO WALL

1/8" CORK

BUTT JOINT

ELEVATION   SCALE 1/2 - 1' - 0   SECTION

Drafting by Mogens Leth

Gottscho-Schleisner

DETAIL OF CORK WALL TREATMENT
AND CONCEALED PERIMETER LIGHTING

DETAIL OF OPEN CEILING AND
LIGHTING PLAN FOR OFFICE AREA

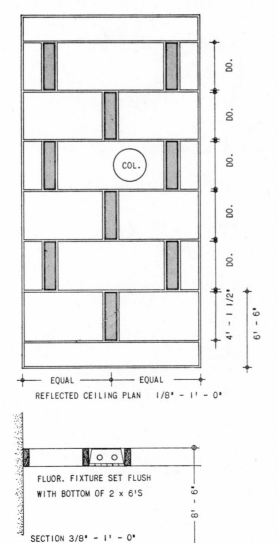

COL.

DO.

DO.

DO.

DO.

DO.

4' - 1 1/2"

6' - 6"

EQUAL   EQUAL

REFLECTED CEILING PLAN   1/8" - 1' - 0"

FLUOR. FIXTURE SET FLUSH
WITH BOTTOM OF 2 × 6'S

8' - 6"

SECTION 3/8" - 1' - 0"

Gottscho-Schleisner

DETAIL OF FOUR PART DISPLAY CASE UNIT

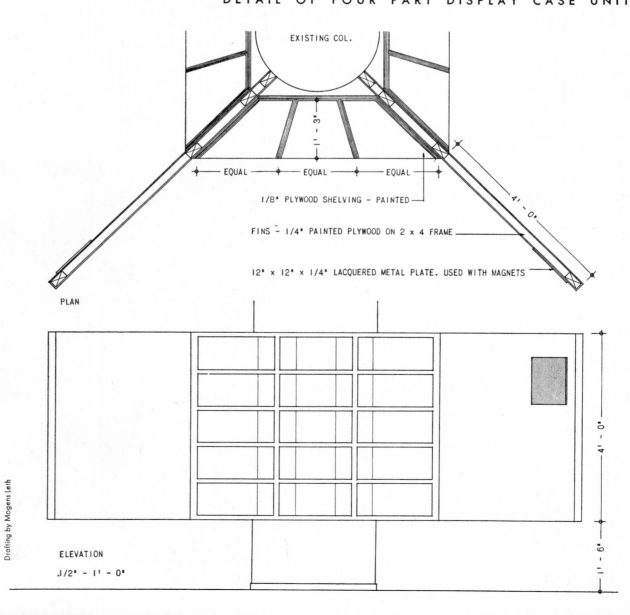

EXISTING COL.

1' - 3'

EQUAL | EQUAL | EQUAL

1/8" PLYWOOD SHELVING - PAINTED

FINS - 1/4" PAINTED PLYWOOD ON 2 x 4 FRAME

12" x 12" x 1/4" LACQUERED METAL PLATE. USED WITH MAGNETS

4' - 0"

PLAN

Drafting by Mogens Leth

ELEVATION

1/2" - 1' - 0"

4' - 0"

1' - 6"

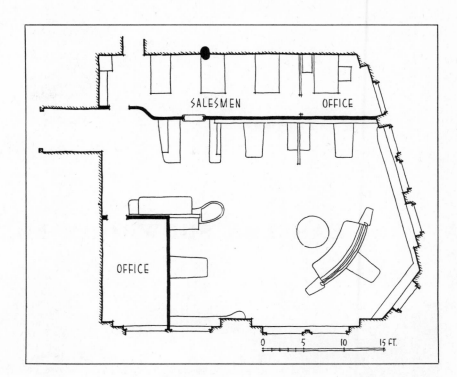

The Bernhard Altmann Corp.
New York, New York
Gerhard E. Karplus, Architect

MULTI-PURPOSE SHOWROOMS AND SALES OFFICE

Ben Schnall

THE INITIAL DIFFICULTIES lay in basic construction — the removal and conversion of several dentists' offices with their complicated plumbing. The client expressly desired that the main showroom reflect the "luxury and romantic background of cashmere," and seem a relaxing living room rather than a place of business. Therefore soft colors, murals and plants were used. The entire floor area was carpeted, the ceiling was furred and acoustically treated, and existing windows are concealed behind continuous drapes.

Receptionist's area with sales cubicles behind it, and the view from the entrance into the main showroom

EASTERN SHOWROOM FOR CALIFORNIA MAKEI

The reception area, above left, is defined by the lighting cove
and the floor treatment; is separated from the sales area proper
by a wood screen against the back of which, right page, are built
two sales desks of natural white birch with plastic work surface

Gerhard E. Karplus

Architect

OF SWIMMING SUITS

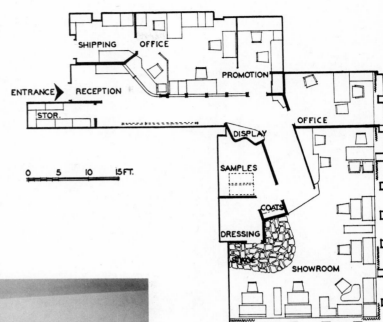

Ben Schnall

THE ARCHITECT for this Broadway showroom had two main problems to tackle in designing the interiors pictured. The owner, Rose Marie Reid, a California manufacturer of beachwear, wanted a large showroom containing five sales booths and desks for two salesmen as well as the necessary ancillary spaces; a private office; a publicity department; and a shipping room — all incorporated into a relatively small area of irregular shape. Another requirement was to capture as much as possible of the light and colorful atmosphere attributed to California. These problems were met by a rather free plan; the attempt to achieve as much of a sense of openness as possible by the use of screens free of floor and ceiling and the selection of net and semi-transparent hangings; and by employing a wide range of delicate colors in high key.

Typical dividers for sales booths consist of an upper display easel formed
of perforated metal painted light gray and a lower cabinet for sample storage built of white birch in natural finish. Tables and chairs are mostly
of stock design, except for the corner units, which are architect designed

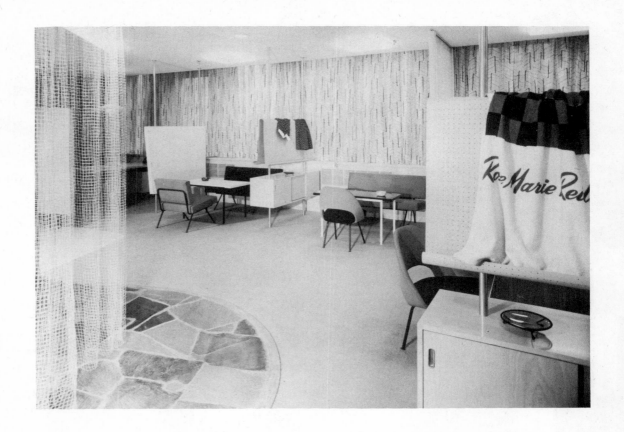

Note the platform for modelling, above and left, which is paved in vari-colored flagstone. Typical window hangings, left and above, are a lightweight black print on white, and are suspended from a continuous track in the recess between ceiling and piers

Ben Schnall

DESIGNED FOR DISPLAY OF HOSPITAL EQUIPMENT

A. S. Aloe Co., Los Angeles

Richard J. Neutra, Architect

ENTIRELY in keeping with the merchandise on display is the hospital-like atmosphere of the new Aloe building in Los Angeles, designed, in the architect's words, "not to compete with, but to form the proper background and foil for" laboratory appliances, surgery tables, etc.

Exterior of the two-story building is stucco with mica glaze, stainless steel and aluminum. Showrooms, a truss-fitting department, general offices, and handling and shipping facilities (not shown on plan) occupy the main floor, stock shelving and warehousing the second.

The large showroom, above and opposite, is actually one room, but is departmentalized by counter placement and stub partitions (see plan, next page). Walls are plywood veneer and laminated plastic, floor is black and gray asphalt tile, ceiling is acoustic tile.

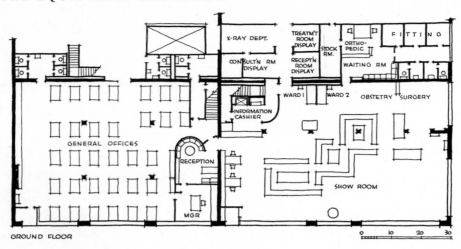

GROUND FLOOR

Julius Shulman Photos

Main touch of color in the showroom is a 60-ft. mural over the wall cases, designed by the architect and executed by Hans Mangelsdorff. It depicts, says Mr. Neutra, ''the subtropical hospital overlooking a bay of the blue-green ocean and a shore of palms and luxurious Henry Rousseau vegetation.'' Significance is the interest of the Aloe Company in the development of health facilities in the Pacific area. Glass-fronted wall cases are lighted from bottom and ceiling; floor cases have glass tops, indexed drawers

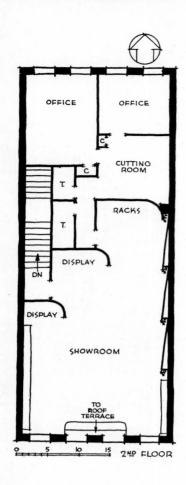

OFFICE   OFFICE

CUTTING
ROOM

RACKS

DISPLAY

DN

DISPLAY

SHOWROOM

TO
ROOF
TERRACE

0   5   10   15   2ND FLOOR

Building facade was defaced with fire escape which could not be removed. New redwood entrance, however, provides vestibule and brightly illuminated show case to identify occupancy

SHOWROOM AND BUILDING FOR CREATIVE LOOMS, INC.

New York City; Marie Frommer, Architect

THIS display room for an exclusive handweaving firm has been planned to provide suitable environment for the display of colorful merchandise. Architect Marie Frommer, achieves the proper atmosphere by means of a soft totally indirect lighting system accented only by recessed spotlights above display areas. In addition great restraint has been used in interior decorative treatment. Walls, ceilings, and floors are not only simple

in form and texture, but are sedately toned in varying shades of warm gray.

The complete architectural task was to convert an existing two-story and basement loft building into offices, showroom, and manufacturing area. Principal remodeling was done on the second floor where the showroom was planned to the south and rear, the cutting room placed in the center, and offices moved to the

Ben Schnall Photos

Bottom of page: Lighting scheme of rhythmically arranged fluorescent strips used in street floor working area is novel for cloth weaving which generally has lights concentrated over each individual loom

north facade. The showroom thus has a pleasant view to the south and convenient access by means of four French doors to a landscaped rear terrace used for outdoor exhibits. A new and comfortable stair provides customers with direct and easy access from the street to showroom.

The street floor is manufacturing area and includes space for all the various procedures involved in the production of handwoven fabrics. Storage is in basement.

CORY SHOWROOM, LOS ANGELES, CALIF.

Maynard Lyndon, Architect

Merge Studios

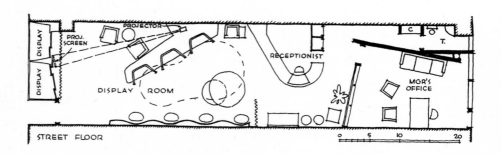

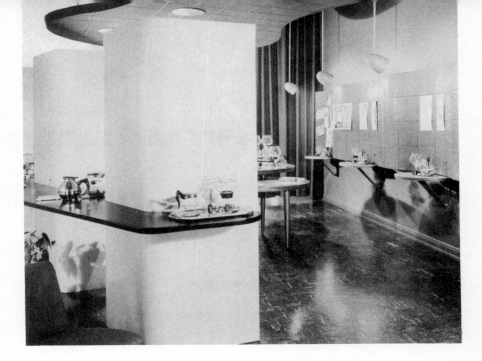

The curving acoustic tile panel is painted dark blue; the wall behind is claret; opposite wall is light blue. Dark green was chosen for the suspended ceiling panel; the high ceiling is yellow. Rear curtain is claret matching wall; front curtain concealing street window display is gray

THE essential planning problem of this dealer's showroom was to provide for the efficient display of current items of manufacturer's equipment and current advertising without alteration of permanent walls, ceiling, doors, or shop front. In solving this problem the architect has created unusually refreshing and original space arrangements and backgrounds through the studied juxtaposition of contrasting geometrical forms.

The principal display area with its most dramatic background — three curved plywood display recesses — has been developed in widening perspective directly off the street entrance. These three plywood recesses, which intersect a continuous black table, have dark blue linings, all other surfaces natural wood. An adjustable display table arrangement, permitted by pivotal small table that swings under large one, is also a feature. Facing the plywood recesses is a curving wall of composition acoustic tile which provides a background for the display of current advertising. Models featured in advertising are shown on small rounded tables cantilevered forward at the lower edge of the tile.

The whole display area, faced and controlled by the large curved receptionist's desk, has a suspended panel ceiling introduced to provide scale and unity and accommodate concealed spotlights.

The space directly to the left of the entrance, behind the principal display features, has been organized for the projection of slides and movies of manufacturing processes, successful sales techniques, etc. Coffee is served in this area.

The long curved receptionist's desk has white linoleum top, natural birch sides. The display fixture at left of desk has built-in mirror to show bottom of equipment. Pivoted tables in center of the display area are natural mahogany. Translucent wall conceals manager's office

"WITH A FINE ITALIAN HAND"

House of Italian Handicraft, New York

Gustavo F. Pulitzer, Architect

OBJECTS displayed in this converted 3-story "brownstone" house are not mass-produced. They are originals done with a fine Italian hand. Most are chosen for special suitability to quantity copying in America, under license, in the manner of a Paris dress.

In keeping with this handicraft aim, so different from the pure quantity-production concept of many American design firms, the architect, Gustavo F. Pulitzer, has relied for background on a hand-tailored curved wall, on mosaic murals, on special materials and devices, rather than a play with simple mass materials such as string and metal bars. Both kinds are contemporary.

The House of Italian Handicraft is an effort to help Italians manage recovery by doing what they do best, not the mass-produced object but the model, highly refined. Display is to the trade. The reception room, seen on these two pages, is important.

The entrance foyer, as seen from the room (right), is largely transparent, does not visually subtract much of the precious space from the room. As seen from within (bottom of page), its plate glass panel is contrived not only as a show window but also as an inviting peep upstairs; while the glass door directs the entrant straight, and pleasantly, to the receptionist

Ben Schnall Photos

Ben Schnall Photos

OFFICES AND SHOWROOMS WITH A SPECIALTY SHOP AIR

Lily of France Corset Company, New York City

Leon and Lionel Levy, Architects

A SPECIALTY shop atmosphere and an unusually compact plan characterize the new headquarters of the Lily of France Corset Company on the fourth floor of a midtown Manhattan office building. The former is achieved through such nice detail as the main entrance (seen above), the latter by grouping offices and small showrooms around a large circular salon which, logically enough, forms the heart of the suite. The entrance is set back from the public corridor much as that of an exclusive small shop might be from the building line, and the wide double doors are given a distinctive air by antique mirrored panels. Plants and flower boxes are used throughout to lend a vivid accent to the predominantly delicate colors of the decorative scheme.

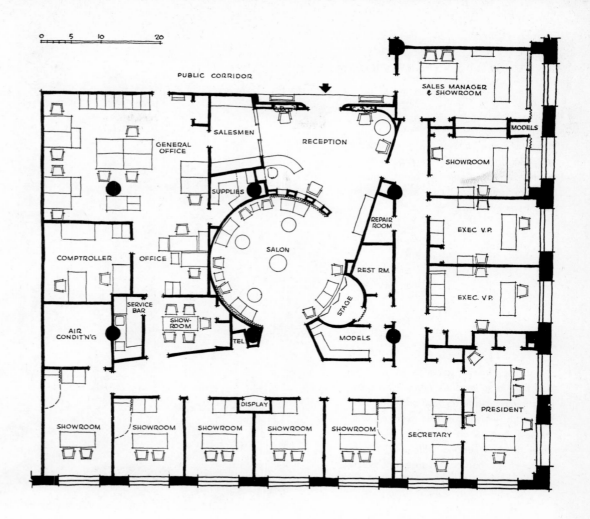

Chief design problem faced by the architects was the economical use of the square floor area, since offices and showrooms had to be both numerous and of varying size. Below: a corner of the reception hall, looking toward the salesmen's room. The partition at right is for decorative purposes only, has no glass in panels

CORSET COMPANY SHOWROOM

Right: the curved plywood wall separating reception hall and salon is pigeon-holed for the decorative value of plants against the beige background. Niches can also be used as special display boxes if desired

Below: the circular salon serves both as reception room and as main showroom, has a built-in stage for fashion shows (left of photo), which connects with models' dressing room. Draperies are pale green, tables of ebony edged with gold, chairs and couches upholstered in green and beige

Above, left: one of the vice presidents' offices has light green papered walls and beige carpets, mahogany furniture. Above, right: the president's office (see plan, page 239) has a large conference table at one end; walls are walnut flexwood, draperies are hand printed. Right: one of the small showrooms; furniture and wood trim are bleached walnut, the Chinese-motif wallpaper is green

The smaller offices and showrooms, one of which is seen at left, are arranged around the periphery of the central salon. All decorated differently, they are tied together by Chinese accents and bleached walnut furnishings. Specially designed glass partitions conceal the building's exterior curtain wall

INDEX

INDEX